What readers are saying about *Groovy Recipes*

This is the go-to guide for turning Groovy into every Java developer's perfect utility knife. Whether you need to quickly parse an Atom feed, serve up an Excel spreadsheet from your Grails app, or create a tarball on the fly, this book will show you how. In true Groovy style, Scott does away with all unnecessary ceremony and gets right down to business. In almost every section, the very first thing you see is code—the recipe for solving the problem at hand—and if you want to stick around for the clear and informative explanation, well, that's strictly optional.

▶ **Jason Rudolph**
Author, *Getting Started with Grails*

Groovy Recipes is the book that I want to have in reach whenever I work in my Groovy bakery. Nothing gets you faster up to speed than having well-thought-out recipes for your everyday tasks.

▶ **Dierk König**
Canoo Engineering AG

The format of this book is ideal for rapidly obtaining crucial information just when you need it. An agile text for agile development!

▶ **Joe McTee**
Software Engineer, JEKLsoft

Groovy is on my radar as one of the next big things in Java, and this book gets you up to speed quickly with lots of great code examples.

▶ **David Geary**
Author, Clarity Training, Inc.

Scott does a fantastic job of presenting many little nuggets of "grooviness" here in a way that is easy to read and follow. There is plenty here for Groovy newcomers and veterans alike. Thanks, Scott!

▶ **Jeff Brown**
Member of the Groovy and Grails Core Development Teams

Adding Groovy to Java is like adding rocket fuel to your SUV. Suddenly everything gets easier, faster, and much more responsive. Scott Davis does his normal excellent job of showing how to do so, and he does it in a clear, simple, and even entertaining way.

▶ **Ken Kousen**
President, Kousen IT, Inc.

This book provides quick examples for your everyday tasks. Don't believe Scott when he says you can read any section in random—the writing is so darn good I could not put the book down until I read it from cover to cover.

▶ **Venkat Subramaniam**
Author, *Programming Groovy*; President, Agile Developer, Inc.

Groovy Recipes
Greasing the Wheels of Java

Groovy Recipes

Greasing the Wheels of Java

Scott Davis

The Pragmatic Bookshelf
Raleigh, North Carolina   Dallas, Texas

Many of the designations used by manufacturers and sellers to distinguish their products are claimed as trademarks. Where those designations appear in this book, and The Pragmatic Programmers, LLC was aware of a trademark claim, the designations have been printed in initial capital letters or in all capitals. The Pragmatic Starter Kit, The Pragmatic Programmer, Pragmatic Programming, Pragmatic Bookshelf and the linking *g* device are trademarks of The Pragmatic Programmers, LLC.

Every precaution was taken in the preparation of this book. However, the publisher assumes no responsibility for errors or omissions, or for damages that may result from the use of information (including program listings) contained herein.

Our Pragmatic courses, workshops, and other products can help you and your team create better software and have more fun. For more information, as well as the latest Pragmatic titles, please visit us at

http://www.pragprog.com

ISBN-10: 0-9787392-9-9

ISBN-13: 978-0-9787392-9-4

Printed on acid-free paper with 50% recycled, 15% post-consumer content.

First printing, January 2008

Version: 2008-1-29

Contents

Preface

Groovy is a successful, powerful, and mature language that all good Java developers should have in their toolboxes. It can be used for making your unit tests more expressive, for scripting tasks such as XML parsing or data imports, for providing extension points in your application where end users can customize the behavior with their own scripts, for defining domain-specific languages to express readable and concise business rules, or even as a full-blown general-purpose language for writing applications from end to end with the Groovy-based Grails web framework.

The main goal of Groovy has always been to simplify the life of developers by providing an elegant language that is easy to learn thanks to its Java-like syntax, but it is also packed with useful features and APIs for all the common programming tasks. Groovy also tries to address the shortcomings of Java by propelling it into the 21st century. You can use Groovy today—without waiting for Java 7, 8, or 9—and benefit from closures; properties; native syntax for lists, maps, and regular expressions; and more.

There are already several books about Groovy—yet another great sign of Groovy's popularity and maturity—but *Groovy Recipes* is unique in that it is the fastest way to get up to speed with the language and to find information on a specific language feature in no time, thanks to its clear structure. But it is not only a bag of tips 'n' tricks, because if you really want to learn about Groovy, there's a story to read, a guiding hand that leads you to enlightenment by progressively teaching you more about the language in a very natural and friendly fashion. To be frank, I've even discovered a couple of tricks I didn't know myself!

Me, Groovy project manager!

I'm sure you'll enjoy this book as much as I did and that you'll keep it on your desk to help you in your everyday developer life. You'll get the job done in no time with *Groovy Recipes* handy.

Guillaume Laforge (Groovy project manager)
January 3, 2008

Chapter 1

Introduction

Once upon a time, Java was the language you *wrote once* and *ran anywhere*. The ability to write code on one operating system (say, OS X) and drop it unchanged onto another (Windows, Solaris, or Linux) ended up being a huge win for users accustomed to waiting for the version that would run on their machine. Before Java, didn't it seem like your operating system was always the last one to be supported?

As we got to know Java better, it turns out that the *platform* (the Java Virtual Machine, or JVM) is what provided the WORA magic, not the *language*. Consequently, we are in the midst of the second Java revolution—one in which Java the language shares the platform with more than 150 other languages.[1] Paradoxically, as Java *the language* loses its monopoly, Java *the platform* is becoming more important than ever.

With so many choices available to us as developers, what makes Groovy stand out from the rest of the crowd? For that matter, why look beyond the venerable Java language in the first place? I can sum it up in one sentence: *Groovy is what Java would look like had it been written in the 21st century.*

Groovy is a new breed of language. It doesn't replace old technology as much as it enhances it. It was created by Java developers who wanted the day-to-day experience of writing code to be simpler. You no longer have to wade through all of that boilerplate code.

---

1. http://www.robert-tolksdorf.de/vmlanguages.html

More important, however, this isn't a "Hey, guys, let's rewrite our entire application from the ground up to take advantage of this new language" approach to software development. No, this is a "Let's use a language that seamlessly integrates with our existing codebase" approach.

Groovy runs on the JVM you already have installed (1.4, 1.5, or 1.6). You write Groovy in the same IDE you use for Java development. You deploy it to the same application servers you already have in production. As a matter of fact, drop a single groovy.jar into your classpath, and you have just "Groovy-enabled" your entire application.

In this book, I hope to show the seasoned Java veteran how easy it is to incorporate Groovy into an existing codebase. I hope to appeal to the busy Java developer by presenting some quick Groovy code snippets that solve everyday problems immediately. ("How do I parse an XML document with namespaces?") But most important, I hope to appeal to the Java developer who is looking to breathe new life into a platform that is more than a dozen years old. Features such as closures, domain-specific languages, and metaprogramming are all now available on a platform that the cool kids seem to have written off as hopelessly behind the times.

Some technical books are *read once*. Then, after you learn the material, the book sits on the shelf gathering dust. If my hunch is correct, this will be one of the *read many* books in your collection, as helpful to you after you become a Groovy master as it was when you read it for the first time.

The reason I think you'll keep reaching for this book is that most *read once* books are written for *sequential access*—in other words, Chapter 7 doesn't make sense unless you've read Chapters 1–6. This book is optimized for *random access*. I've tried to lay it out in a way that you will reach for it again and again, knowing you can quickly scan the table of contents to find the snippet of code you need. Each section is a stand-alone entity with plenty of breadcrumbs to point you to related topics.

Having a PDF of this book on my laptop during the course of writing has proven valuable more than once. If a PDF could get dog-eared, mine would be nearly threadbare. Being able to electronically search for either a code fragment or a phrase—right there in a window next to my text editor—is absolutely priceless. It has changed the way I write Groovy, and I had years of experience with the language before I started writing the book!

1.1 Groovy, the Way Java Should Be

Groovy was expressly designed to appeal to Java developers. Groovy *is* Java at the end of the day. The other languages that run on the JVM are just that—*other* languages. The point of JRuby[2] is to get existing Ruby code running on the JVM. The point of Jython[3] is to get existing Python code running on the JVM. The point of Groovy is to integrate with your existing *Java* code.

I'm not trying to diminish the value of those other languages. If you already have an existing codebase implemented in another language, the benefits are undeniable. But how do they benefit Java developers with an existing Java codebase? Groovy and Java are so compatible that in most cases you can take a Java file—foo.java—and rename it to foo.groovy. You will have a perfectly valid (and executable) Groovy file. That trick won't work with any of your other neighbors on the JVM.

But more than language-level compatibility, Groovy allows you to dramatically reduce the amount of code you would normally write in Java. For example, let's start with a simple Java class named Person.java that has two attributes, firstName and lastName. As Java developers, we are trained from a tender young age to create public classes with private attributes. All outside access to the attributes is routed through public getters and setters.

```java
/** Java Code */
public class Person {
  private String firstName;
  private String lastName;

  public String getFirstName() {
    return firstName;
  }

  public void setFirstName(String firstName) {
    this.firstName = firstName;
  }

  public String getLastName() {
    return lastName;
  }

  public void setLastName(String lastName) {
    this.lastName = lastName;
  }
}
```

---

2. http://jruby.codehaus.org/
3. http://www.jython.org

I'm not arguing with established Java practices. Encapsulation offers many benefits. Unfortunately, it comes with a heavy verbosity tax.

It took us more than twenty lines of code to define a class that has two attributes. Each new attribute will cost us six more lines of code for boilerplate getters and setters. The fact that modern IDEs will generate the requisite getters and setters for us doesn't make the problem go away; it makes the symptoms only slightly less painful.

What does the corresponding Groovy class look like? You can rename Person.java to Person.groovy and the file will compile, but it is hardly idiomatic Groovy.

What Java developers first notice about Groovy is its brevity. Good Groovy code is Java boiled down to its essence. You can see this immediately in the Groovy version of the Person class:

```
/** Groovy Code */
class Person {
  String firstName
  String lastName
}
```

Yes, that's all there is. Even better, it's a drop-in replacement for the Java class. Compile it down to bytecode, and the Groovy version is indistinguishable from its Java counterpart. You'll need to have groovy.jar in your classpath, but with that in place your Java code can seamlessly call any plain old Groovy object (POGO) in lieu of a POJO with the same name and fields.

All POGOs are public by default. All attributes are private. There are getters and setters for each field, but these methods are autogenerated in the bytecode rather than the source code. This drops the 6:1 code ratio for new fields down to exactly 1:1. Looking at this POGO compared to the Java class, there is nothing more that could be left out. It is the core of the POJO with all the syntactic noise stripped away.

Of course, you could slowly begin adding Java language features back in one by one.

You could certainly use semicolons if you prefer. You could explicitly say public class Person and private String firstName. There is nothing stopping you from having getters and setters in your source code.

Recall that you could literally rename Person.java to Person.groovy and still have syntactically correct Groovy. But after you see the simple elegance of the Groovy version, why would you want to add all that complexity back in?

1.2 Stripping Away the Verbosity

Let's explore this verbosity issue some more. Consider the canonical "Hello World" example in Java:

```
public class HelloWorld {
  public static void main(String[] args) {
    System.out.println("Hello World");
  }
}
```

Groovy scripts implicitly create the public class line as well as the public static void main() line, leaving you with this for the drop-in replacement:

```
println "Hello World"
```

Again, both are bytecode compatible and fully interchangeable. The Groovy example does exactly what the Java code does but with a fraction of the lines of code.

As one final example, how many lines of Java would it take for you to open a simple text file, walk through it line by line, and print the results? By my count, it's about thirty-five lines of code:

```
import java.io.BufferedReader;
import java.io.FileNotFoundException;
import java.io.FileReader;
import java.io.IOException;

public class WalkFile {
  public static void main(String[] args) {
    BufferedReader br = null;
    try {
      br = new BufferedReader(new FileReader("../simpleFile.txt"));
      String line = null;
      while((line = br.readLine()) != null) {
        System.out.println(line);
      }
    }
    catch(FileNotFoundException e) {
      e.printStackTrace();
    }
    catch(IOException e) {
      e.printStackTrace();
    }
```

```
      finally {
        if(br != null) {
          try {
            br.close();
          }
          catch(IOException e) {
            e.printStackTrace();
          }
        }
      }
    }
  }
}
```

I'm not suggesting that line count is the only thing you should be considering. If that were your only concern, you could shorten this example by importing java.io.* instead of each class explicitly. You could move some of the shorter catch blocks up to a single line for brevity's sake.

No, the concern you should have about this code is the baked-in verbosity. Here is the corresponding Groovy code:

```
new File("../simpleFile.txt").eachLine{line ->
  println line
}
```

If you wanted to play loose and fast with styling rules, you could have a one-liner that is a drop-in replacement for the thirty-five lines in the Java example. The line count is simply one example of what I like about Groovy—the fact that I can see the forest for the trees is a real benefit. The fact that the Groovy code I write is a drop-in replacement for Java is another. For these reasons, I like thinking of Groovy as "executable pseudocode."

1.3 Groovy: The Blue Pill or the Red Pill?

In the sci-fi movie *The Matrix*, the main character—Neo—is presented with two choices. If he takes the blue pill, he will return to his everyday life. Nothing changes. If, however, he chooses the red pill, he'll be granted a whole new perspective on the world. He'll get superhero powers. (He chooses the red pill, of course. It wouldn't be much of a movie if he didn't.)

Groovy offers you two paths as well.

The "blue pill" usage of Groovy simply makes Java easier to use. As the Person class example illustrated, Groovy can be used as a drop-in replacement for Java without changing any of the semantics of the Java language. This should appeal to conservative organizations.

In "red pill" mode, Groovy introduces new language constructs that are different from Java. File.eachLine is a *closure*—it is a whole new way to iterate over a file without using java.util.Iterator. Closures are being considered for inclusion in Java 1.7, yet you have them right here, right now. This should appeal to folks who are envious of cool features in other languages, wishing Java could do similar things.

Perhaps James Strachan said it best on August 29, 2003, when he introduced the world to a little open source project he had been working on. In a blog entry[4] titled "Groovy: The Birth of a New Dynamic Language for the Java Platform," he said this:

"Dynamically typed languages like Ruby and Python are getting quite popular it seems. I'm still not convinced we should all move to dynamically typed languages any time soon—however, I see no reason why we can't use both dynamically and statically typed languages and choose the best tool for the job.

"I've wanted to use a cool dynamically typed scripting language specifically for the Java platform for a little while. There's plenty to choose from, but none of them quite feels right—especially from the perspective of a die-hard Java programmer. Python and Ruby are both pretty cool—though they are platforms in their own right. I'd rather a dynamic language that builds right on top of all the groovy Java code out there and the JVM.

"So I've been musing a little while if it's time the Java platform had its own dynamic language designed from the ground up to work real nice with existing code, creating/extending objects normal Java can use, and vice versa. Python/Jython [is] a pretty good base—add the nice stuff from Ruby and maybe sprinkle on some AOP features, and we could have a really groovy new language for scripting Java objects, writing test cases, and, who knows, even doing real development in it."

That is how Groovy got both its name and its worldview. Groovy is a language that takes on the characteristics you'd like it to take on. Traditional Java development made easier or a way to get all those exciting new features from other languages onto the JVM? The answer is both.

---

4.   http://radio.weblogs.com/0112098/2003/08/29.html

1.4 Road Map

You can read this book in several ways. Each chapter focuses on a particular topic such as XML, file I/O, web services, or metaprogramming. To get a solid overview of the subject and how Groovy can help you, simply read the chapter from start to finish like you would any other book.

However, if you are in a hurry and have a specific problem you need to fix, the table of contents is your friend. Each chapter is divided into sections that solve a specific problem or describe a specific language feature: "Listing all files in a directory," "Reading the contents of a file," "Writing text to a file," and so on. Each section starts with a block of code, ready for you to type it in and go about your business. Read on if you need a bit more explanation. I've tried to make each section as independent as possible. If it uses features described elsewhere, the sections are judiciously cross-referenced in a way that you should be comfortable wherever you dive in.

Chapter 2, *Getting Started*, on page 13 shows how to install Groovy, how to compile Groovy code, and how to Groovy-enable a text editor or IDE.

Chapter 3, *New to Groovy*, on page 31 is a "red pill" chapter, showing experienced Java developers all the interesting new features Groovy brings to the party: duck typing, Groovy truth, and closures.

Chapter 4, *Java and Groovy Integration*, on page 59 is a "blue pill" chapter, demonstrating how Groovy can be integrated with an existing Java infrastructure.

Chapter 5, *Groovy from the Command Line*, on page 77 takes you someplace you might not have considered Java a good match for: the command line. Groovy makes a heck of a shell-script replacement, which allows you to leverage all the familiar Java idioms and libraries for system administration tasks.

Chapter 6, *File Tricks*, on page 91 demonstrates the different ways you can use Groovy to work with the filesystem: listing files in a directory, reading files, copying them, and so forth.

Chapter 7, *Parsing XML*, on page 107 shows how easy XML can be to work with in Groovy. You can parse XML documents, getting at elements and attributes with ease.

Chapter 8, *Writing XML*, on page 127 shows the flip side of the XML coin: writing out XML documents. You'll learn about everything from simple XML marshaling to creating complex XML documents with declarations, processing instructions, CDATA blocks, and more.

Chapter 9, *Web Services*, on page 143 brings remote systems into play. We will explore making SOAP calls, RESTful calls, XML-RPC calls, and more.

Chapter 10, *Metaprogramming*, on page 173 explores a new way of thinking about programming on the JVM. Dynamically discovering existing classes, fields, and methods quickly leads to creating new classes and methods on the fly, as well as adding new functionality to existing classes all at runtime.

Chapter 11, *Working with Grails*, on page 193 introduces a full-featured web framework that is built atop familiar Java libraries such as Spring and Hibernate but that uses Groovy as the dynamic glue to hold everything together.

Chapter 12, *Grails and Web Services*, on page 227 shows how to use Grails for more than returning simple HTML. We'll look at RESTful web services, JSON web services, Atom feeds, podcast feeds, and more.

1.5 Acknowledgments

Thanks once again to Dave Thomas and Andy Hunt for creating the Pragmatic Bookshelf. This is my second book with them, and I continue to be pleasantly surprised at what a developer-friendly publishing company they have put together, both as an author and an avid reader of their titles.

This is also my second time around with Daniel Steinberg at the helm as my editor. He took my semi-lucid vision of writing a *code-first* Groovy book and, against all odds, coaxed out what you are holding in your hands right now. His one-word comments of "Huh?" and "Why?" and "Really?" gently nudged me toward expanding on ideas where I was too terse, warming up the prose where it was too clinical, and offering justifications and my real-world experiences where the curly braces and semicolons weren't enough. It was a real joy working with him, and I'm truly looking forward to our next project together.

A warm thank you goes out to my fearless posse of technical review-ers. Their keen eyes and sharp tongues kept me humble and my code tight. The comments from Groovy project leader Guillaume Laforge and Grails project leader Graeme Rocher were as shrewd and timely as you might expect. Project committers Jeff Brown, Dierk Koenig, and Jason Rudolph graciously shared their insider knowledge, while David Geary, Ken Kousen, Joe McTee, and Greg Ostravich made sure that my exam-ples were intelligible to folks not already waist-deep in the language. A special thank you goes to my good friend Venkat Subramaniam—we started working on this book together and then quickly realized that two books were better than one. His strategic take on the language in *Learning Groovy* is the perfect complement to the tactical approach I take here.

Big thanks go to Jay Zimmerman, founder of the No Fluff, Just Stuff symposium tour. He recognized early on what a gem Groovy is to the Java development community and has actively supported it ever since. He paid for professional development on the language until G2One was formed by Graeme, Guillaume, and Alex Tkachman to take over. Groovy and Grails presentations are featured prominently in the NFJS lineup, and the 2G Experience—the first North American conference dedicated to Groovy and Grails—continues to demonstrate his firm commitment to broadening the language's appeal. I've worked closely with Jay since 2003, and there has never been a dull moment.

Finally, my family deserves my deepest gratitude. While they often bear the brunt of my odd writing schedule and ever-present deadlines, they rarely complain about it—at least not to my face. My wife, Kim, doles out seemingly bottomless portions of patience and encouragement, and it does not go unnoticed. Her two most frequent questions during the writing of *Groovy Recipes* were "Are you done with the book yet?" and "When are you going to write something that I want to read?" I can answer "Yes...finally" to one and "Soon...I hope" to the other. Young Christopher was very supportive of the writing process as long as it didn't preempt our Norman Rockwellian walks to and from kinder-garten or our time together on the Nintendo Wii. (I made sure that it didn't.) And young Elizabeth, now toddling and tall enough to reach the doorknob to Daddy's office at home, made sure that I didn't go too long without a big smile and an infectious giggle or two. Much love to each of you.

Chapter 2

Getting Started

Installing Groovy is just as easy as installing Ant, Tomcat, or Java itself—unzip the distribution, create an environment variable, and ensure that the binaries are in your PATH. Once Groovy is in place, you can run it in any number of ways—compiled or uncompiled, from the shell or a GUI console, or from the command line or a web server. If you have two minutes (or less!), you have enough time to begin experimenting with Groovy. This chapter will have you up and running before you can say "next-generation Java development."

2.1 Installing Groovy

1. Download and unzip groovy.zip from http://groovy.codehaus.org.
2. Create a GROOVY_HOME environment variable.
3. Add $GROOVY_HOME/bin to the PATH.

Everything you need to run Groovy is included in a single ZIP file—well, everything except the JDK, that is. Groovy 1.x runs on all modern versions of Java—1.4, 1.5, and 1.6. If you are running an older version of Java, cruise by http://java.sun.com for an update. If you don't know which version of Java you have installed, type java -version at a command prompt:

```
$ java -version
===>
java version "1.5.0_13"
Java(TM) 2 Runtime Environment, Standard Edition (build 1.5.0_13-b05-237)
Java HotSpot(TM) Client VM (build 1.5.0_13-119, mixed mode, sharing)
```

To take advantage of Java 1.5 language features such as annotations and generics in Groovy, it probably goes without saying that you'll need at least a 1.5 JDK under the covers.

Groovy runs noticeably faster on each new generation of the JVM, so unless there is something else holding you back, my recommendation is to run Groovy on the latest and greatest version of Java that you can.

Similarly, I recommend running the latest version of Groovy that you can. Groovy 1.0 was released in January 2007. The next major release, Groovy 1.5, shipped in December 2007. You'll see how to determine which version of Groovy you are running in a moment.

The Groovy development team took great pains to ensure that basic syntax and interfaces stayed consistent between Groovy 1.0 and 1.5. The jump in version numbers signified two things: the addition of Java 5 language features and the huge jump in stability and raw performance. If you are still running Groovy 1.0, most of the examples in this book will run unchanged. The ExpandoMetaClass class was added in Groovy 1.5, but metaprogramming has been an integral part of the language since the very beginning. The examples in Chapter 10, *Metaprogramming*, on page 173 that don't specifically use an ExpandoMetaClass class will behave the same way in either version of Groovy. The bottom line is that all 1.*x* versions of Groovy should be reasonably interchangeable. Breaking syntax changes are reserved for Groovy 2.*x* and beyond.

I've included information on how install Groovy with a section on the specifics for Windows and another on the details for the Unix, Linux, Mac OS X family.

Checking the Groovy Version

```
$ groovy -version
Groovy Version: 1.5.0 JVM: 1.5.0_13-119
```

You can tell which version of Groovy you have installed by typing groovy -version at a command prompt. As shown here, this command shows the Java version as well.

Installing Groovy on Unix, Linux, and Mac OS X

Download the latest Groovy ZIP file from http://groovy.codehaus.org. Unzip it to the directory of your choice. I prefer /opt. You will end up with a groovy directory that has the version number on the end of it, such as groovy-1.5. I like creating a symlink that doesn't include the specific version number: ln -s groovy-1.5 groovy. This allows me to switch between versions of Groovy cleanly and easily.

Since ZIP files don't preserve Unix file permissions, be sure to swing by the bin directory and make the files executable:

```
$ chmod a+x *
```

Once the directory is in place, you next need to create a GROOVY_HOME environment variable. The steps to do this vary from shell to shell. For Bash, you edit either .bash_profile or .bash_rc in your home directory. Add the following:

```
### Groovy
GROOVY_HOME=/opt/groovy
PATH=$PATH:$GROOVY_HOME/bin
export GROOVY_HOME PATH
```

For these changes to take effect, you need to restart your terminal session. Alternately, you can type source .bash_profile to load the changes into the current session. You can type echo $GROOVY_HOME to confirm that your changes took effect:

```
$ echo $GROOVY_HOME
/opt/groovy
```

To verify that the Groovy command is in the path, type groovy -version. If you see a message similar to this, then you have successfully installed Groovy:

```
Groovy Version: 1.5.0 JVM: 1.5.0_13-119
```

Installing Groovy on Windows

Download the latest Groovy ZIP file from http://groovy.codehaus.org. Unzip it to the directory of your choice. I prefer c:\opt. You will end up with a groovy directory that has the version number on the end of it, such as groovy-1.5. Although you can rename it to something simpler such as groovy, I've found that keeping the version number on the directory name helps make future upgrades less ambiguous.

Once the directory is in place, you next need to create a GROOVY_HOME environment variable. For Windows XP, go to the Control Panel, and double-click System. Click the Advanced tab and then Environment Variables at the bottom of the window. In the new window, click New under System Variables. Use GROOVY_HOME for the variable name and c:\opt\groovy-1.5 for the variable value.

To add Groovy to the path, find the PATH variable, and double-click it. Add ;%GROOVY_HOME%\bin to the end of the variable. (Do not forget the leading semicolon.) Click OK to back your way out of all the dialog boxes. For these changes to take effect, you need to exit or restart any command prompts you have open. Open a new command prompt, and type set to display a list of all environment variables. Make sure that GROOVY_HOME appears.

To verify that the Groovy command is in the path, type groovy -version. If you see a message similar to this, then you have successfully installed Groovy:

```
Groovy Version: 1.5.0 JVM: 1.5.0_13-119
```

2.2 Running a Groovy Script (groovy)

```
// hello.groovy
println "Hello Groovy World"

$ groovy hello.groovy
$ groovy hello
===> Hello Groovy World
```

One of the first things experienced Java developers notice about Groovy is that they can run the code without compiling it first. You just type and go—much more like writing JSP pages than Java classes. This might lead you to believe that Groovy is an interpreted language. In reality, Groovy is compiled into bytecode just like Java. The groovy command both compiles and runs your code. You won't, however, find the resulting .class file laying around anywhere. The bytecode is created in memory and discarded at the end of the run. (If you want those class files to stick around, see Section 2.3, *Compiling Groovy (groovyc)*, on the facing page.)

On-the-fly bytecode compilation means that Groovy can offer an interactive shell. Typing commands and seeing them execute immediately is the quickest way to experiment with the language. For more on this, see Section 2.4, *Running the Groovy Shell (groovysh)*, on the next page. The drawback, of course, is that your code goes away once the shell closes. The shell is great for experimentation, but you'll want to create Groovy scripts if you want to do anything more than quick-and-dirty playing around.

To create a Groovy script, create a new text file named hello.groovy. Add the following line:

```
println "Hello Groovy World"
```

Save the file, and then type groovy hello.groovy at the command prompt. Since you gave it a .groovy file extension, you can also type just groovy hello. Congratulations! You are now officially a Groovy developer. Welcome to the club.

For more on running uncompiled Groovy, see Chapter 5, *Groovy from the Command Line*, on page 77.

2.3 Compiling Groovy (groovyc)

```
$ groovyc hello.groovy

// on Unix, Linux, and Mac OS X
$ java -cp $GROOVY_HOME/embeddable/groovy-all-1.5.0.jar:. hello
===> Hello Groovy World

// on Windows
$ java -cp %GROOVY_HOME%/embeddable/groovy-all-1.5.0.jar;. hello
===> Hello Groovy World
```

If you are trying to run just a quick script, letting the groovy command compile your code on the fly makes perfect sense. If, however, you are trying to intermingle your Groovy classes with your legacy Java classes, the groovyc compiler is the only way to go. As long as the Groovy JAR is on your classpath, your Java classes can call Groovy as easily as Groovy classes can call Java.

For more on compiling Groovy and integrating with Java classes, see Chapter 4, *Java and Groovy Integration*, on page 59.

2.4 Running the Groovy Shell (groovysh)

```
$ groovysh

Groovy Shell (1.5.0, JVM: 1.5.0_13-119)
Type 'help' or '\h' for help.
----------------------------------------
groovy:000> println "Hello Groovy World"
Hello Groovy World
===> null
```

The Groovy shell allows you to work with Groovy interactively. There is no need to create a file or compile anything—simply type groovysh at the command prompt, and begin typing Groovy statements such as println "Hello Groovy World". The results will appear each time you press the Enter key. To exit the Groovy shell, type exit.

That null message is nothing to worry about. It just means that the last command you typed didn't return a value. Had you typed something like 2+2, the message would be the result of the statement: 4. The last line of a method in Groovy is an implicit return statement, and the Groovy shell behaves the same way:

```
groovy:000> 2+2
===> 4
groovy:000> s = "John"
===> John
groovy:000> s.toUpperCase()
===> JOHN
groovy:000> s.each{println it}
J
o
h
n
===> John
```

The toUpperCase() method comes straight from the java.lang.String class. For more on the each closure, see Section 3.14, *Iterating*, on page 49.

The Groovy shell stores a history of everything you've typed—even after you exit the shell. You can use the up and down arrow keys to quickly reenter commands or correct a fat-fingered syntax error.

The :000 at the prompt indicates how many lines of Groovy code have been typed without being run. For example, you can define a class on the fly in the Groovy shell and use it right away. (Of course, the class goes away once you exit the shell.)

```
groovy:000> class Person{
groovy:001>    String name
groovy:002>    String toString(){
groovy:003>       "Hi! My name is ${name}"
groovy:004>    }
groovy:005> }
===> true
groovy:000> p = new Person(name:"John")
===> Hi! My name is John
```

Did you notice that you didn't see null either time? The first time you get a true—that's the Groovy shell's way of saying, "OK, I was able to define that class for you." The second time you see the toString output of the class. At the risk of sounding a bit cheeky, you'll quickly learn to pay attention to the Groovy shell's results only when you care about what it has to say....

Gotcha: Why Does the Groovy Shell Forget Your Variables?

```
groovy:000> String s = "Jane"
groovy:000> println s
===>
ERROR groovy.lang.MissingPropertyException:
No such property: s for class: groovysh_evaluate

groovy:000> s = "Jane"
groovy:000> println s
===> Jane
```

The Groovy shell has a curious case of amnesia when It comes to typed variables. A variable declared with either a datatype or a def is forgotten immediately. An untyped variable is remembered for the duration of the shell session. This can be a source of great confusion when copying code into the shell from a script—in the script the code is fine, whereas in the shell it is broken.

To make sense of this apparent discrepancy, you need to better understand how the Groovy shell is implemented. (If you feel your eyes beginning to glaze over, just leave the type declarations off your shell variables, and move along....)

The Groovy shell is an interactive instance of a groovy.lang. GroovyShell. This class is also what enables the evaluate command discussed in Section 5.10, *Evaluating a String*, on page 86. Each GroovyShell stores locally declared variables (such as s = "Jane") in a groovy.lang.Binding.

This Binding object is essentially the "big hashmap in the sky." When you type println s, the shell calls binding.getVariable("s") behind the scenes. Variables declared with a datatype (String s = "Jane") don't get stored in the Binding, so they can't be found the next time you ask for them.

For more on the GroovyShell and Binding objects, see Section 10.4, *Discovering the Methods of a Class*, on page 180.

Figure 2.1: THE GROOVY CONSOLE

Finding Class Methods on the Fly

```
groovy:000> String.methods.each{println it}
public int java.lang.String.hashCode()
public volatile int java.lang.String.compareTo(java.lang.Object)
public int java.lang.String.compareTo(java.lang.String)
public boolean java.lang.String.equals(java.lang.Object)
public int java.lang.String.length()
...
```

You can use the Groovy shell to quickly discover all the methods on a given class. For example, let's say you want to see all the String methods. The previous example does the trick.

The nice thing about asking a class directly for its methods is that it is always up-to-date—Javadocs, on the other hand, can easily get out of sync with the live code. For more on class introspection, see Chapter 10, *Metaprogramming*, on page 173.

At the beginning of this section, we discussed the null message that can be safely ignored if a command has no output. Unfortunately, this is another example of shell output that is more noise than information.

The command String.methods.each{println it} returns an error after successfully displaying all the methods on the class:

```
groovy:000> String.methods.each{println it}
...
public final native void java.lang.Object.notify()
public final native void java.lang.Object.notifyAll()
ERROR groovy.lang.MissingMethodException:
No signature of method:
org.codehaus.groovy.tools.shell.Groovysh$_closure1.call()
is applicable for argument types:
...
```

Remember when I said that you'll quickly learn to pay attention to the Groovy shell's results only when you care about what it has to say? After all the methods are displayed, the shell tries to execute the result of the String.methods call (and fails spectacularly, I might add). Since I'm used to seeing it, the error doesn't bother me a bit. I ignore it since I know that it is going to happen, and after all, this *is* ad hoc code. If the error message bothers you, you can add a statement to the end of the call that evaluates correctly, such as String.methods.each{println it}; "DONE". You'll be typing a few extra characters, but you'll avoid the wrath of an angry shell as well.

Getting Help

```
groovy:000> help
For information about Groovy, visit:
    http://groovy.codehaus.org

Available commands:
  help      (\h) Display this help message
  ?         (\?) Alias to: help
  exit      (\x) Exit the shell
  quit      (\q) Alias to: exit
  import    (\i) Import a class into the namespace
  display   (\d) Display the current buffer
  clear     (\c) Clear the buffer
  show      (\S) Show variables, classes or imports
  inspect   (\n) Inspect a variable or the last result
                 with the GUI object browser
  purge     (\p) Purge variables, classes, imports or preferences
  edit      (\e) Edit the current buffer
  load      (\l) Load a file or URL into the buffer
  .         (\.) Alias to: load
  save      (\s) Save the current buffer to a file
  record    (\r) Record the current session to a file
  history   (\H) Display, manage and recall edit-line history
  alias     (\a) Create an alias
  set       (\=) Set (or list) preferences
```

```
For help on a specific command type:
    help command
```

Typing help while in the Groovy shell brings up some nice little hidden gems. import behaves just as it does in Java source code, allowing you to work with classes in other packages. If you are in the middle of defining a long class and mess up, clear returns you to a :000 state. To wipe an entire session clean, typing purge gets you back to the state you were in when you first started the shell. record saves everything you type to a file, allowing you to "play it back" later. history shows what the shell remembers you typing in.

2.5 Running the Groovy Console (groovyConsole)

```
$ groovyConsole
```

In addition to a text-based Groovy shell, Groovy also provides a graphical console. (See Figure 2.1, on page 20.) Type commands in the upper half of the window. Choose Script > Run, and look for the results in the bottom half. (Choosing Script > Run Selection allows you to narrow your focus to just the highlighted lines of code.)

The Groovy shell discussed in Section 2.4, *Running the Groovy Shell (groovysh)*, on page 17 appeals to command-line cowboys. The Groovy console is meant to attract the more refined GUI crowd—those who have grown accustomed to the niceties of Cut/Copy/Paste, Undo/Redo, and so on. The console is no replacement for a true text editor, but it offers a few more amenities than the shell. For example, if you have an existing Groovy script, you can open it in the console by choosing File > Open. You can also save a shell session by choosing File > Save.

You even have a graphical object browser to get a deeper look into fields and methods available on a given class. The last object from the console run is an instance of Person. Choose Script > Inspect Last to snoop around, as shown in Figure 2.2, on the facing page.

2.6 Running Groovy on a Web Server (Groovlets)

```
1. Copy $GROOVY_HOME/embeddable/groovy.jar to WEB-INF/lib.
2. Add groovy.servlet.GroovyServlet to WEB-INF/web.xml.
3. Place your Groovy scripts wherever you'd normally place your JSP files.
4. Create hyperlinks to your Groovy scripts.
```

Adding a single Groovy servlet to your web application gives you the ability to run uncompiled Groovy scripts on the server.

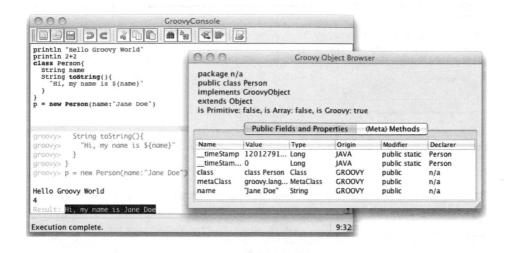

Figure 2.2: THE GROOVY OBJECT BROWSER

The Groovy servlet acts like the groovy command on the command line—it compiles your .groovy scripts on the fly.

To get started, copy groovy.jar from $GROOVY_HOME/embedded into the WEB-INF/lib directory of your JEE application. This Groovy-enables your entire web application. To run Groovlets on the fly, add the groovy.servlet. GroovyServlet entry to the WEB-INF/web.xml deployment descriptor. You can map whatever URL pattern you'd like, but *.groovy is the usual mapping.

```
<web-app version="2.4"
    xmlns="http://java.sun.com/xml/ns/j2ee"
    xmlns:xsi="http://www.w3.org/2001/XMLSchema-instance"
    xsi:schemaLocation="http://java.sun.com/xml/ns/j2ee web-app_2_4.xsd">

    <servlet>
        <servlet-name>Groovy</servlet-name>
        <servlet-class>groovy.servlet.GroovyServlet</servlet-class>
    </servlet>

    <servlet-mapping>
        <servlet-name>Groovy</servlet-name>
        <url-pattern>*.groovy</url-pattern>
    </servlet-mapping>

    <!-- The Welcome File List -->
    <welcome-file-list>
        <welcome-file>index.jsp</welcome-file>
    </welcome-file-list>
</web-app>
```

Hello Scott

Figure 2.3: A FRIENDLY GROOVLET

You can now drop any uncompiled Groovy script into your web directory, and it will run. For example, create a file named hello.groovy in the root of your web application directory. Add the following line:

```
println "Hello ${request.getParameter('name')}"
```

This Groovlet echoes whatever you pass in via the name parameter. To test it, visit http://localhost:8080/g2/hello.groovy?name=Scott in a web browser. The friendly Groovlet should say "Hello" in a personalized way. (See Figure 2.3.)

You can easily create hyperlinks to your Groovlets, just as you would any other file type:

```
<a href="http://localhost:8080/g2/hello.groovy?name=Scott">Say Hello</a>
```

The Groovlet can also handle form submissions. Notice that the form method is GET and the field name is name. This will create the same URL you typed by hand and put in the hyperlink earlier. For a slightly more advanced Groovlet, see Section 10.3, *Checking for the Existence of a Field*, on page 177.

```
<html>
  <body>
    <form method="get" action="hello.groovy">
      Name: <input type="text" name="name" />
      <input type="submit" value="Say Hi" />
    </form>
  </body>
</html>
```

Web Server Status-Check Groovlet

```
// stats.groovy
html.h1("Disk Free (df -h)")
html.pre('df -h'.execute().text)
html.hr()
html.h1("IP Config (ifconfig)")
html.pre('ifconfig'.execute().text)
```

```
html.hr()
html.h1("Top (top -1 1)")
html.pre('top -1 1'.execute().text)
```

This is a common Groovlet that I have deployed to many of my web
servers. It allows me to see, at a glance, some of the key statistics that
help me judge the health of the server—the amount of disk space free,
the network settings, the current processes running on the server, and
so on.

Normally I'd ssh into the machine and type these various commands
at the command prompt. Instead, I can visit http://localhost:8080/stats.
groovy and get the same results. Any command that would normally be
typed by hand can be surrounded in quotes and executed by Groovy
on my behalf. (For more on this, see Section 5.4, *Running a Shell Command*, on page 80.) Next, I can wrap those results in HTML fragments
using the MarkupBuilder named html that is available to every Groovlet.
(For more on this, see Section 8.13, *Creating HTML on the Fly*, on
page 137.)

Here is what the resulting HTML looks like...

```
<h1>Disk Free (df -h)</h1>
<pre>Filesystem     Size  Used  Avail Capacity  Mounted on
/dev/disk0s2    149Gi 113Gi  36Gi    76%     /
devfs           107Ki 107Ki   0Bi   100%     /dev
fdesc           1.0Ki 1.0Ki   0Bi   100%     /dev
map -hosts        0Bi   0Bi   0Bi   100%     /net
map auto_home     0Bi   0Bi   0Bi   100%     /home
</pre>
<hr />
<h1>IP Config (ifconfig)</h1>
<pre>lo0: flags=8049&lt;UP,LOOPBACK,RUNNING,MULTICAST&gt; mtu 16384
        inet6 fe80::1%lo0 prefixlen 64 scopeid 0x1
        inet 127.0.0.1 netmask 0xff000000
        inet6 ::1 prefixlen 128
gif0: flags=8010&lt;POINTOPOINT,MULTICAST&gt; mtu 1280
stf0: flags=0&lt;&gt; mtu 1280
en0: flags=8863&lt;UP,BROADCAST,SMART,RUNNING,SIMPLEX,MULTICAST&gt; mtu 1500
```

...but, more important, in Figure 2.4, on the next page, you can see
what it looks like in the browser.

Groovlets aren't meant to be a replacement for a full-feature web framework. They are simply scripts that you can run on a web server as easily
as you could from the command line. For an example of using Groovy
within a web framework, see the chapters on Grails and Gorm.

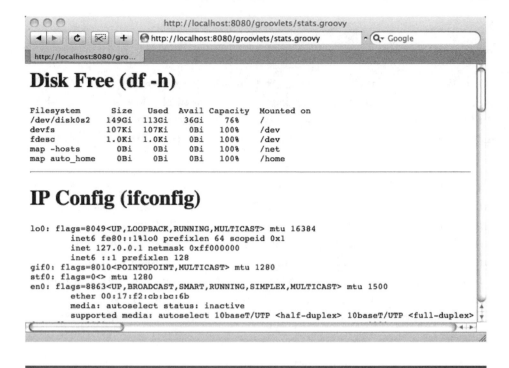

Figure 2.4: A GROOVLET SHOWING SERVER STATISTICS

2.7 Groovy + Eclipse

http://groovy.codehaus.org/Eclipse+Plugin

If you are using Eclipse 3.2 or newer, there is a Groovy plug-in that provides the same IDE support (code completion, syntax highlighting, debugging) you've come to expect for Java.

Installing the Plug-In

To install the Groovy/Eclipse plug-in, follow these steps:

1. Choose Help > Software Updates > Find and Install > Search for New Features.

2. Click New Remote Site.

3. Type Groovy in the Name field.

4. Type http://dist.codehaus.org/groovy/distributions/update/ in the URL field, and click OK.

5. Check the Groovy repository, and click Finish.

6. Select Groovy under Select Features to Install, and click Next.

7. Read the agreement, and click Next.

8. Set the default location, and click Finish.

9. If you get a warning about the plug-in being unsigned, don't worry. Click Install.

Restart Eclipse, and you should be ready to use Groovy.

Starting a New Groovy Project

To start a new Groovy project, follow these steps:

1. Choose File > New > Project.

2. Choose Java Project, and click Next.

3. Type the name of your choice in the Project Name field.

4. Select Create Separate Source and Output Folders, and then click Finish.

5. In the Package Explorer, right-click your project, and then choose Groovy > Add Groovy Nature.

Finally, you will want to change the output folder for your compiled Groovy code:

1. In the Package Explorer, right-click your project, and choose Build Path > Configure Build Path.

2. Change the Default Output Folder from bin to bin-groovy.

2.8 Groovy + IntelliJ IDEA

http://www.jetbrains.com/idea/

IntelliJ IDEA 7.*x* offers native support for Groovy and Grails. Code completion, syntax highlighting, refactoring support, and more are all standard features. (See Figure 2.5, on the following page.) Look for the Jet-Groovy plug-in if it's not installed by default.

If you have IntelliJ IDEA 6.*x*, the GroovyJ plug-in will at least give you rudimentary syntax highlighting. To install it, pull up the Preferences screen, and click the Plugins button. Select GroovyJ from the list, and click OK.

```
    void testInheritFromInterfaceHeirarchy() {
        new File("").e
    }                     m  ⌐ each (Closure p1)              void
                          m  ▯ eachByte (Closure p1)          void
}                         m  ▯ eachDir (Closure p1)           void
                          m  ▯ eachDirMatch (Object p1, Closure p2)  void
import groovy.sw m  ▯ eachDirRecurse (Closure p1)      void
import groovy.sw m  ▯ eachFile (Closure p1)            void
                          m  ▯ eachFileMatch (Object p1, Closure p2) void
interface IBar { m  ▯ eachFileRecurse (Closure p1)     void
interface Foo ex m  ▯ eachLine (Closure p1)            void
```

Figure 2.5: CODE COMPLETION IN INTELLIJ IDEA 7.*x*

2.9 Groovy + TextMate

http://macromates.com/
http://macromates.com/wiki/Main/SubversionCheckout
http://groovy.codehaus.org/TextMate
http://www.e-texteditor.com/

TextMate is a popular text editor for the Mac. It offers pluggable language support through its Bundle system.

Check out the Groovy bundle (Groovy.tmbundle) from the Macromates Subversion repository. Copy the file to ~/Library/Application Support/ TextMate/Bundles. Restart TextMate, and Groovy should appear under the Bundles menu.

The Groovy TextMate wiki page lists other Groovy-related bundles, including bundles for Grails and GANT (a Groovy implementation of Ant).

You can also create your own from scratch using the Bundle Editor. Choose Bundles > Bundle Editor > Show Bundle Editor. (See Figure 2.6, on the next page.)

Windows users might want to check out E Text Editor. It promises the "power of TextMate on Windows." TextMate bundles are supposed to work in E Text Editor as well.

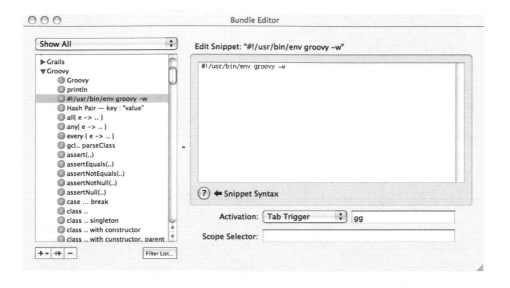

Figure 2.6: TEXTMATE'S BUNDLE EDITOR

2.10 Groovy + (Insert Your IDE or Text Editor Here)

http://groovy.codehaus.org/Other+Plugins

There is Groovy support available for nearly every modern IDE and text editor. For details on NetBeans, XCode, TextPad, SubEthaEdit, Vim, Emacs, and others, check out the Other Plugins page on the Groovy wiki.

Another good source for information is your friendly neighborhood search engine. For example, typing groovy xcode, groovy vi, or groovy [your IDE] into a search engine yields a number of hits from various people who have blogged about their successes (as well as their stumbling blocks, of course).

Chapter 3

New to Groovy

Groovy is meant to complement Java, augment it, and in some cases give it a much needed face-lift. (Java was, after all, released way back in 1995. That's pre-Cambrian in software years, isn't it?) For example, some things that are required in Java are optional in Groovy: semicolons, datatypes, and even exception handling. Groovy automatically includes many more packages than Java does by default. Groovy adds new convenience methods to existing classes such as String, List, and Map. All of this is done to smooth out some of the speed bumps that have historically slowed down the Java development process.

What is most interesting about Groovy is that you've been writing it all along without even realizing it. Valid Java is valid Groovy about 99% of the time—simply rename your .java file to .groovy, and you are ready to run. (See Chapter 4, *Java and Groovy Integration*, on page 59 for the few edge cases that keep Java from being 100% valid Groovy.) Groovy is a superset of Java. It is in no way meant to replace Java. In fact, Groovy would not exist without Java. Groovy is meant to be a better Java than Java, while all along supporting your legacy codebase.

But Groovy does more than improve the existing language. Groovy introduces new classes such as Closure, Range, and GString. Groovy introduces the concept of safe dereferencing to avoid lengthy null-checking blocks. Groovy offers heredocs—a new special multiline String variable. Overall, Groovy "embraces and extends" Java in a positive way. Read on to see what Java would look like if it had been written in the 21st century.

3.1 Automatic Imports

```
import java.lang.*;
import java.util.*;
import java.net.*;
import java.io.*;
import java.math.BigInteger;
import java.math.BigDecimal;

import groovy.lang.*;
import groovy.util.*;
```

Java automatically imports the java.lang package for you. This means you can use classes such as String and Integer and call System.out.println() without having to type import java.lang.* at the top of every Java file.

In Groovy, you get a number of additional packages. In other words, you can use classes from these packages without having to explicitly import them at the top of your file. The net effect of these automatic imports is that much more of the JDK and GDK is available to you by default. Java classes—along with their Groovy enhancements—such as List (Section 3.14, *List Shortcuts*, on page 48), Map (Section 3.15, *Map Shortcuts*, on page 52), File (Chapter 6, *File Tricks*, on page 91), and URL (Chapter 9, *Web Services*, on page 143) are *just there* when you need them. Additionally, common Groovy classes such as XmlParser and XmlSlurper (Section 7.2, *Understanding the Difference Between XmlParser and XmlSlurper*, on page 108), Expando (Section 10.9, *Creating an Expando*, on page 186), and ExpandoMetaClass (Adding Methods to a Class Dynamically (ExpandoMetaClass), on page 190) are ready and waiting for you thanks to the automatic importing that Groovy does on your behalf.

3.2 Optional Semicolons

```
msg = "Hello"
msg += " World"; msg += "!";
println msg;
===> "Hello World!"
```

In Groovy, semicolons are completely optional. You must use them if you have many statements on the same line. Otherwise, using them at the end of a line with a single statement is now a stylistic decision instead of a compiler requirement.

This, of course, means we should get ready for our next big technological holy war. "O Semicolon, Semicolon! Wherefore art thou, Semicolon?"

Sneaking Toward DSLs

```
def list = []
list.add("Groovy")
list.add "Groovy"
list << "Groovy"
```

All three of these statements are equivalent. Each adds the word *Groovy* to the list. The first uses the traditional Java add() method. The second calls the same method, only without the parentheses. The third uses operator overloading (as discussed in Section 3.7, *Operator Overloading*, on page 40). The << operator calls the add() method under the covers. Whether you favor one syntax over the others is a matter of personal preference. In each case, Groovy is trying to make your code as expressive and easy to read as possible while still leaving you with something that will actually execute.

One of the benefits of using a dynamic language such as Groovy is that it makes it easy to create domain-specific languages (DSLs).* Features such as optional parentheses (Section 3.3, *Optional Parentheses*, on the following page) and optional semicolons (Section 3.2, *Optional Semicolons*, on the preceding page) give developers the tools to make programming feel, well, less like programming. A DSL could be viewed as "executable pseudocode." You could also view it as a way to allow nonprogrammers to do simple programming tasks.

```
def shoppingList = []
def add = shoppingList.&add
def remove = shoppingList.&remove
add "Milk"
add "Bread"
add "Beer"
remove "Beer"
add "Apple Juice"
print shoppingList
```

In addition to leaving out parentheses and semicolons, this trivial example uses method pointers (Section 10.7, *Creating a Method Pointer*, on page 185) to further simplify the syntax. Very quickly, you have something that doesn't feel like writing source code at all. add "Milk", remove "Beer", and print shoppingList all feel very natural to write, even for nonprogrammers.

Continued on next page.

---

*. http://en.wikipedia.org/wiki/Domain-specific_programming_language

---

Sneaking Toward DSLs (cont.)

Compare this with the Java alternative: "Don't forget to include semicolons at the end of every line. *Semicolons*. Like the thing in between the hour and the minutes in '3:00,' only with a dot on top of a comma instead of two dots. You found it—it's right next to the L key on the keyboard. OK, now let's move on to public static void main(String[] args)...."

The best thing about DSLs is that they don't just offer benefits to beginners and nonprogrammers—simplifying source code is an easy win for everyone involved.

I'm tired of arguing about where the opening curly brace should go— if it's good enough for Kernighan and Ritchie,[1] then it's good enough for me. The VIctor of the text editor war[2] has been decided as far as I am concerned. You can have your Emacs—I have a VIable alternative. (Although some people say behind my back that I am a VIctim of an old VIce, I won't dignify those VIcious rumors with a response.)

So, where does that leave us when it comes to optional semicolons? I personally don't use them and quite frankly don't miss them. I think that if they aren't truly required, then they are little more than visual clutter—a vestigial tail that echoes Groovy's past rather than dictates its future. Once you get bitten by the DSL bug (see the sidebar on the previous page), the opportunity to leave off unpronounceable symbols in favor of a more English-like programming style is a welcome change. (Of course, I am always willing to have you buy me a beer and try to show me the error of my ways. Be forewarned—it might take several pints to convince me otherwise....)

3.3 Optional Parentheses

```
println("Hello World!")
println "Hello World!"
===> "Hello World!"
```

---

1. http://en.wikipedia.org/wiki/Indent_style
2. http://en.wikipedia.org/wiki/Editor_war

Parentheses surrounding method arguments are optional in Groovy. This is commonly used for simple methods such as println. However, you must still use the parentheses if a method has no arguments. For example:

```
def s = "Hello"
println s.toUpperCase()
===> HELLO
```

No-argument methods require parentheses because otherwise the compiler would not be able to tell the difference between method calls and the abbreviated getter/setter calls discussed in Section 4.2, *Getter and Setter Shortcut Syntax*, on page 62. After working with Groovy for a while, when you see person.name in code, you'll *just know* that it is a Groovy shortcut for the call to person.getName().

How to Make No-Arg Method Parentheses Optional

Of course, if this whole "no-arg parentheses" requirement really keeps you awake at night, there are a couple of clever ways to get around it. (And no, "switching to Ruby" is not one of the options I'm going to suggest.)

The first workaround is creating a method that looks like a getter, even if it's not truly a getter at all. I'm not a proud man—I've been known to write methods such as getDeliver() on my Pizza class just so that I can call pizza.deliver later. Granted, this breaks the holy "getter/setter" contract that you were all required to sign as neophyte Java developers, but why have rules if you don't break 'em every once in a while?

Another option for getting around those pesky empty parentheses is creating a method pointer, as discussed in Section 10.7, *Creating a Method Pointer*, on page 185:

```
def pizza = new Pizza()
def deliver = pizza.&deliver()
deliver
```

When to Use Parentheses and When to Omit Them

Now that you've decided whether you are going to use semicolons, you face the challenge of figuring out when to use parentheses.

My advice to you is the same as Supreme Court Justice Potter Stewart's: you'll know it when you see it.[3] Doesn't println "Hello" just seem better than System.out.println("Hello")? I can't tell you why—it just *does*.

But that doesn't mean that I avoid parentheses at all times. I probably use them more than I don't. If I'm writing a DSL (as discussed in the sidebar on page 33), I tend to use fewer parentheses. If I'm writing more traditional Java/Groovy code, I'll use them more often. But at the end of the day, I don't have a hard and fast decision-making process other than "at this moment, leaving the parentheses off seems like the right thing to do."

3.4 Optional Return Statements

```
String getFullName(){
    return "${firstName} ${lastName}"
}

//equivalent code
String getFullName(){
    "${firstName} ${lastName}"
}
```

The last line of a method in Groovy is an implicit return statement. We can explicitly use the return statement or safely leave it off.

So, why are return statements optional? Uh, because Al Gore said that all of that extra unnecessary typing is the 623rd leading cause of global warning. "Save the keystrokes, save the planet" isn't just a catchy slogan that I made up on the spot. (Actually it is, but don't you agree that it looks like something you'd see in *An Inconvenient Truth*?)

Just like all of the other optional things in this chapter, allowing you to leave off return statements is an effort to cut down on the visual noise of the programming language. Creating a method such as add(x,y){ x + y } strikes me as the right balance of terseness while still being readable. If it strikes you as too terse, then don't use it. Really. It's OK.

I find myself using return statements if I need to prematurely exit a method. For example, I am a big believer in *failing fast*, so return "Insufficient funds -- try again later." will appear as soon as possible in my withdraw() method. If I use return early in the method, I'll probably use it on the last line as well for visual symmetry. On the other hand, return

---

3. http://en.wikipedia.org/wiki/I_know_it_when_I_see_it

doesn't add much clarity to quick little one-liner methods such as the add method in the previous paragraph. The bottom line is that Groovy allows me to program with intent instead of making me cave in to the peer pressure of the compiler. I'll use return when I'm darn good and ready to, not because the compiler is nagging me to do so.

3.5 Optional Datatype Declaration (Duck Typing)

```
//In scripts:
w = "Hello"
String x = "Hello"
println w.class
===> java.lang.String
println w.class == x.class
===> true

//In compiled classes:
def y = "Hello"
String z = "Hello"
println y.class
===> java.lang.String
println y.class == z.class
===> true
```

Groovy does not force you to explicitly define the type of a variable. def name = "Jane" is equivalent to String name = "Jane"—both are Strings. The keyword def means, "I don't much care what type this variable is, and you shouldn't either." Notice that in scripts and the Groovy shell (as opposed to compiled classes), you can be even more cavalier and leave off the def entirely. In fact, in the Groovy shell you *should* leave off the datatype declarations. (See the sidebar on page 19 for more information.)

Java, on the other hand, is a statically typed language. This means you must give each variable a datatype when you declare it:

```
Duck mallard = new Mallard();
```

In this code snippet, you can't tell whether Duck is a class or an interface. (Think List list = new ArrayList() versus ArrayList list = new ArrayList().) Perhaps Duck is a parent class of Mallard. Perhaps it is an interface that defines the behavior of a Duck. If the compiler allows you to stuff a Mallard into a Duck-shaped variable, then Mallard must offer all the same methods as a Duck. Regardless of how Mallard is actually implemented, you can safely say—at the very least—that Mallard is of type Duck.

This concept is called *polymorphism*—Greek for "many shapes." Polymorphism is the fuel that runs popular dependency injection (DI) frameworks such as Spring, HiveMind, and Google Guice. These DI engines allow developers to keep their classes loosely coupled. For example, if you hard-code references to the MySQL JDBC driver throughout your code, you have to embark on an extensive search-and-replace mission if you later decide to switch to PostgreSQL. On the other hand, java.sql.Driver is an interface. You could simply code to the Driver interface and allow Spring to *inject* the proper JDBC driver implementation at runtime.

Groovy is written in Java, so by extension all variables have a specific datatype. The difference in Groovy is that you aren't forced to explicitly declare the datatype of a variable before using it. In quick-and-dirty scripts, this means you can simply write w = "Hello". You can tell that w is truly of type java.lang.String, can't you? When compiling your Groovy with groovyc, you must use the def keyword if you want to declare a variable without being explicit about the type.

Why is this important? It's not just to save you a few precious keystrokes here and there. It's important because it moves Groovy from being a statically typed language to a dynamically typed one. Objects in dynamically typed languages don't have to satisfy the "contract" of the interface at compile time; they simply have to respond correctly to method calls at runtime. (See Section 10.3, *Checking for the Existence of a Field*, on page 177 and Section 10.5, *Checking for the Existence of a Method*, on page 182 for examples of this.)

```
def d = new Duck()
```

Alex Martelli, author of several best-selling Python books, coined the phrase *duck typing*[4] to describe dynamically typed languages. Your variable doesn't have to be formally declared of type Duck as long as it "walks" like a Duck and "quacks" like a Duck—in other words, it must respond to those method calls at runtime.

3.6 Optional Exception Handling

```
//in Groovy:
def reader = new FileReader("/foo.txt")
```

---

4. http://en.wikipedia.org/wiki/Duck_typing

```
//in Java:
try{
  Reader reader = new FileReader("/foo.txt")
}
catch(FileNotFoundException e){
  e.printStackTrace()
}
```

In Java, there are two types of exceptions: checked and unchecked. Checked exceptions extend java.lang.Exception. We have to wrap methods that might throw an exception in a try/catch block. For example, the FileReader constructor will throw a FileNotFoundException if you pass in a filename that doesn't exist. Unchecked exceptions extend java.lang.Error or java.lang.RuntimeException. Exceptions such as NullPointerException, ClassCastException, and IndexOutOfBoundsException might be thrown by a method, but the compiler doesn't require you to wrap them in a try/catch block. The Javadoc for java.lang.Error says that we don't need to catch these sorts of exceptions "since these errors are abnormal conditions that should never occur."

Although it's nice that Java allows this subtle sort of distinction between checked and unchecked exceptions, it's unfortunate that we the developers don't get to decide the level of severity for ourselves. If the FileReader constructor throws a checked exception and you decide that it's not important enough to catch, the compiler will respectfully disagree with you and refuse to compile your code.

```
$ javac TestFile.java
TestFile.java:6: unreported exception java.io.FileNotFoundException;
must be caught or declared to be thrown
    Reader reader = new FileReader("/foo.txt");
1 error
```

But what if you just explicitly created the file on the previous line? When is the last time a file creation failed for you? Is it a 95% likely occurrence? 5%? 0.0005%? Is it analogous to a SunSetException (something that happens every day) or a SunJustExplodedException? In other words, is it something that you *expect* to happen or something that *just might* happen ("abnormal conditions that should never occur")?

What if you've been writing to that file all along and now you simply want to read the contents back in? Does FileNotFoundException make any sense here at all? What if you're trying to get a handle to a directory that *always* exists on your operating system, such as /etc/hosts or c:\windows? Even though the compiler has the best of intentions, a simple one-line command now takes six lines of code.

And even more insidiously, what do you think that the catch block now contains? If you answered, "Nothing," "Whatever my IDE generated," or "The bare minimum to get that stupid compiler to shut up," you are correct.

Glenn Vanderburg says, "Bad developers will move Heaven and Earth to do the *wrong* thing." But what about benign neglect—simply *accepting the code that your IDE autogenerates* (which is most likely an empty block with a todo tag)?

I apologize if I am kicking the shins of your favorite sacred cow. I appreciate the *intent* of checked exceptions, but I shudder at the thought of how many empty catch blocks are running in production right now, how many developers catch Exception as a regular practice, and how many exceptions are eaten and never rethrown with the misguided intent of keeping the application up and running at all costs.

Now consider how much code out there is dedicated to the dreaded (yet unchecked) NullPointerException. I get nulls on a regular basis, yet the compiler classifies this as an "abnormal condition that should never occur." Clearly there is a gap between the intent and the reality of checked and unchecked exceptions.

Groovy solves this by converting all checked exceptions to unchecked exceptions. This one small move returns the decision of how severe an exception is back to the developer. If you are running a web service that frequently gets malformed requests from the end user, you might choose to catch NullPointerException explicitly, even though the Java compiler doesn't require it. If you're referring to a file that can't possibly be missing (WEB-INF/web.xml, for example), you can choose not to catch FileNotFoundException. The definition of "abnormal conditions that should never occur" is now back fully in your control, thanks to Groovy. As with optional commas and parentheses, you're programming with intent. You're catching an exception because you want to, not because the compiler wants you to do so.

3.7 Operator Overloading

```
def d = new Date()
===> Sat Sep 01 13:14:20 MDT 2007

d.next()
===> Sun Sep 02 13:14:20 MDT 2007
```

```
(1..3).each{ println d++ }
===>
Sat Sep 01 13:14:20 MDT 2007
Sun Sep 02 13:14:20 MDT 2007
Mon Sep 03 13:14:20 MDT 2007
```

Operator overloading is alive and well in Groovy after a long absence from the Java language. As you can see in this example, the ++ operator calls the next() method under the covers. The following list shows the operator and the corresponding method call:

Operator	Method
a == b or a != b	a.equals(b)
a + b	a.plus(b)
a - b	a.minus(b)
a * b	a.multiply(b)
a / b	a.div(b)
a % b	a.mod(b)
a++ or ++a	a.next()
a-- or --a	a.previous()
a & b	a.and(b)
a | b	a.or(b)
a[b]	a.getAt(b)
a[b] = c	a.putAt(b,c)
a << b	a.leftShift(b)
a >> b	a.rightShift(b)
a < b or a > b or a <= b or a >= b	a.compareTo(b)

This syntactic sugar shows up throughout the GDK[5] (Groovy enhancements to the JDK). For example, Section 3.14, *List Shortcuts*, on page 48 demonstrates some convenience operators added to java.util.List. You can add items to a List in the traditional Java way (list.add("foo")) or in the new Groovy way (list << "foo").

Of course, you can add these methods to your own classes as well. order.leftShift(item) becomes order << item in Groovy.

It's up to you whether you use operator overloading, but I have to admit that date + 7 feels a whole lot more natural than date.roll(Calendar.DATE, 7) ever did.

---

5. http://groovy.codehaus.org/groovy-jdk/

3.8 Safe Dereferencing (?)

```
def s = "Jane"
s.size()
===> 5

s = null
s.size()
Caught: java.lang.NullPointerException: Cannot invoke method size()
        on null object at CommandLine.run(CommandLine.groovy:2)

//notice that we can call size()
//without throwing a NullPointerException
//thanks to the safe dereferencing ? operator
s?.size()
===> null
```

Null references can appear unexpectedly. Since they are both common and expensive (throwing an exception halts operation in Java), many Java programmers are in the habit of programming defensively around potentially null situations like this:

```
if(s != null){
  s.doSomething();
}
```

This is tedious (and verbose) if receiving a null reference isn't as catastrophic as the compiler would like you to believe. Groovy offers a shortcut if you'd like to ignore the NullPointerException and proceed silently. Put a question mark at the end of any potentially null object reference, and Groovy will wrap the call in a try/catch block for you behind the scenes.

```
s?.doSomething()
```

This safe dereferencing can be chained to any depth. Suppose you have a Person class that has an Address class that has a PhoneNumber class. You can safely drill all the way down to the phone number without worrying about trapping for each individual *potential* NullPointerException.

```
//in Java:
if(person != null && person.getAddress() != null
          && person.getAddress().getPhoneNumber() != null ){
  System.out.println(person.getAddress().getPhoneNumber());
}
else{
  System.out.println("");
}

//in Groovy:
println person?.address?.phoneNumber
```

3.9 Autoboxing

```
def i = 2
println i.class
===> java.lang.Integer

def d = 2.2
println d.class
===> java.math.BigDecimal
```

Autoboxing helps overcome a peculiarity of the Java language: Java is object-oriented, except when it isn't. Java offers primitive datatypes (int, float, double) as well as objects (Integer, Float, Double). In 1995, this was a reasonable concession. Primitives were used for speed; objects were used for developer convenience. When Java 5 was released, Sun added autoboxing (transparently promoting primitives to its Uppercase Brethren) to help smooth over this historical oddity. Sun didn't eliminate the primitive/object divide; it just made it less readily apparent.

Groovy takes Java 5 autoboxing one step further—it autoboxes everything on the fly. This means you can perform interesting tasks such as calling methods on what looks like a primitive to a Java developer's eye:

```
2.class
===> class java.lang.Integer

2.toFloat()
===> 2.0

3.times{println "Hi"}
Hi
Hi
Hi
```

Even if you explicitly cast a variable as a primitive, you still get an object. In Groovy, *everything* is an Object. Everything. Primitives no longer exist as far as Groovy is concerned.

```
float f = (float) 2.2F
f.class
===> class java.lang.Float
```

What about calling a Java method that expects a primitive instead of an object? No worries—Groovy unboxes these values as needed. If you want more precise control over this, you can use the as keyword:

```
javaClass.javaMethod(totalCost as double)
```

If you explicitly cast a number to a float or a double, it'll get autoboxed to a Float or a Double. If you just type a number with a decimal place, it'll get autoboxed to a BigDecimal. Why is this? Well, it's primarily to avoid the dreaded "floating-point arithmetic" bugaboo in Java:

```
//In Java:
public class PiggyBank{
  public static void main(String[] args){
    double sum = 0.0d;
    for(int i = 0; i < 10; i++){
      sum += 0.1d;
    }
    System.out.println(sum);
  }
}


$ java PiggyBank
===> 0.9999999999999999
```

Let's say you put a dime in your piggy bank for ten days in a row. According to Java, do you end up with a dollar or with something that asymptotically *approaches* a dollar without ever really getting there?

Joshua Bloch has an entire section devoted to this in his seminal book *Effective Java*. On page 149, the title of Item 31 says it all: "Avoid float and double if exact answers are required." How does Groovy handle the same problem?

```
//In Groovy:
def sum = 0
10.times{ sum += 0.1}
println sum
===> 1.0
```

The Javadoc for java.math.BigDecimal states that it is best used for "immutable, arbitrary-precision signed decimal numbers. The BigDecimal class gives its user complete control over rounding behavior." The principle of least surprise suggests that 1.1 + 1.1 ought to return 2.2 and 10 * 0.1 should equal 1.0. BigDecimal (and Groovy) gives you the results you expect.

3.10 Groovy Truth

```
//true
if(1)        // any non-zero value is true
if(-1)
if(!null)    // any non-null value is true
if("John")   // any non-empty string is true
```

```
Map family = [dad:"John", mom:"Jane"]
if(family)    // true since the map is populated

String[] sa = new String[1]
if(sa)        // true since the array length is greater than 0

StringBuffer sb = new StringBuffer()
sb.append("Hi")
if(sb)        // true since the StringBuffer is populated

//false
if(0)         // zero is false
if(null)      // null is false
if("")        // empty strings are false

Map family = [:]
if(family)    // false since the map is empty

String[] sa = new String[0]
if(sa)        // false since the array is zero length

StringBuffer sb = new StringBuffer()
if(sb)        // false since the StringBuffer is empty
```

"Groovy truth" is shorthand for what evaluates to true in the Groovy language. In Java, the only thing that evaluates to true is, well, true. This can lead to lots of extraneous typing. For example, if you are trying to pull in a command-line argument in Java, you must do the following:

```
//in Java:
if(args != null && args.length > 0){
  File dir = new File(args[0]);
}
else{
  System.out.println("Usage: ListDir /some/dir/name");
}
```

Granted, you could simply write File dir = new File(args[0]) and hope for the best. But what if your user doesn't supply the correct number of parameters? What if they type java ListDir instead of java ListDir /tmp? Which error do you prefer that they see?

```
//default message:
Exception in thread "main" java.lang.ArrayIndexOutOfBoundsException: 0
        at ListDir.main(ListDir.java:6)

//your custom error message:
Usage: ListDir /some/dir/name
```

Thanks to Groovy truth, that same error-trapping code block can be shortened to this:

```
//in Groovy:
if(args){
  dir = new File(args[0])
}
else{
  println "Usage: ListDir /some/dir/name"
}
```

0, NULL, and "" (empty strings) all evaluate to false. This means a simple if(args) catches all the most likely things you want to avoid when processing input from the user.

3.11 Embedded Quotes

```
def s1 = 'My name is "Jane"'
def s2 = "My name is 'Jane'"
def s3 = "My name is \"Jane\""
```

Groovy adds some nice new tricks to Java Strings. In Java, a single quote is used to represent a single char primitive. In Groovy, we can use single quotes to surround a String. This means we can use single quotes to hold a String that has embedded double quotes without having to escape them. The same, of course, is true of double-quoted Strings that contain embedded single quotes. Escaping characters with a backspace is the same in both languages.

3.12 Heredocs (Triple Quotes)

```
String s = """This is a
multi-line String.
"You don't need to escape internal quotes", he said.
"""

def ss = '''This
That, The Other'''

def xml = """
<book id="987">
  <title>Groovy Recipes</title>
  <author>Scott Davis</author>
</book>"""

def html = """<body onload="init()">...</body>"""
```

Heredocs[6] are available in many dynamic languages, from Python to Perl to Ruby. A heredoc allows you to store multiline Strings in a single variable. Groovy uses triple quotes (three single quotes or three double quotes) to define heredocs.

Even if your Strings are single-lined, heredocs are still quite valuable. Dropping snippets of XML, HTML, or JSON into a variable is a great strategy for unit testing. Not having to escape internal quotes makes it easy to copy a bit of output into a variable and immediately begin writing assertions against it.

For a real-world example of heredocs in action, see Section 12.4, *Setting Up an Atom Feed*, on page 233.

3.13 GStrings

```
def name = "John"
println "Hello ${name}. Today is ${new Date()}"
===> Hello John. Today is Fri Dec 28 15:16:32 MDT 2007
```

Embedded dollar signs and curly braces inside Strings are a familiar sight to anyone who works with Ant build files or Java Server Pages (JSPs). It makes String concatenation much easier than traditional Java: "Hello " + name + ".". Groovy brings this syntax to the language in the form of GStrings (short for "Groovy strings," of course). Any String with an embedded expression is a GString:

```
println "Hello John".class
===> class java.lang.String
```

```
println "Hello ${name}".class
===> class org.codehaus.groovy.runtime.GStringImpl
```

Mixing GStrings with heredocs (Section 3.12, *Heredocs (Triple Quotes)*, on the facing page) makes for an especially powerful combination:

```
def name = "John"
def date = new Date()
def amount = 987.65
def template = """
Dear ${name},
   This is a friendly notice that ${amount} was
   deposited in your checking account on ${date}.
"""
```

---

6. http://en.wikipedia.org/wiki/Heredoc

3.14 List Shortcuts

```
def languages = ["Java", "Groovy", "JRuby"]
println languages.class
===> java.util.ArrayList
```

Groovy offers a concise syntax for creating ArrayLists.

Put a comma-delimited list of values in square brackets to the right of the equals sign, and you have a List. (Maps offer a similarly easy construct—see Section 3.15, *Map Shortcuts*, on page 52.)

Although square brackets will give you an ArrayList by default, you can put an as clause on the end of the line to coax out various other datatypes. For example:

```
def languages = ["Java", "Groovy", "JRuby"] as String[]
def languages = ["Java", "Groovy", "JRuby"] as Set
```

Creating an Empty List

```
def empty = []
println empty.size()
===> 0
```

To create an empty List, simply use the empty set notation.

Adding an Element

```
def languages = ["Java", "Groovy", "JRuby"]
languages << "Jython"
===> [Java, Groovy, JRuby, Jython]
```

Adding items to a List is easy. Groovy overloads the << operator to the leftShift() method to accomplish this. (For more on operator overloading, see Section 3.7, *Operator Overloading*, on page 40.)

Getting an Element

```
def languages = ["Java", "Groovy", "JRuby"]
println languages[1]
println languages.getAt(1)
==> Groovy
```

Even though languages is technically a List, you can make array-like calls to it as well. Groovy blurs the syntactic distinction between Lists and Arrays, allowing you to use the style that is most pleasing to you.

Iterating

```
def languages = ["Java", "Groovy", "JRuby"]

//using the default 'it' variable:
languages.each{println it}
===>
Java
Groovy
JRuby

//using the named variable of your choice:
languages.each{lang ->
  println lang
}
===>
Java
Groovy
JRuby
```

Iterating through a List is such a common activity that Groovy gives you a convenient way to do it. In the first example, you use the default name for the iterator variable, it. In the second example, you explicitly name the variable lang.

Of course, all the traditional Java ways of iterating over a List are still available to you. If you like the Java 5 for..in syntax or java.util.Iterator, you can continue to use it. Remember that Groovy augments Java; it doesn't replace it.

Iterating with an Index

```
def languages = ["Java", "Groovy", "JRuby"]
languages.eachWithIndex{lang, i ->
  println "${i}: ${lang}"
}
===>
0: Java
1: Groovy
2: JRuby
```

eachWithIndex() gives you both the current element and a counter variable.

Sort

```
def languages = ["Java", "Groovy", "JRuby"]
languages.sort()
===>  [Groovy, JRuby, Java]
println languages
===>  [Groovy, JRuby, Java]
```

You can easily sort a List. Note that this is a permanent change. sort() modifies the internal sort order of the original List.

Reverse

```
def languages = ["Java", "Groovy", "JRuby"]
languages.reverse()
===> [JRuby, Groovy, Java]
println languages
===> [Java, Groovy, JRuby]
```

You can easily reverse a list. Note that reverse() does not modify the original sort order of the List. It returns a new List.

Pop

```
def languages = ["Java", "Groovy", "JRuby"]
languages.pop()
===> "JRuby"
println languages
===> [Java, Groovy]
```

You can pop things off the List. The pop method uses LIFO, meaning *last in, first out*. Note that this is a permanent change. pop() removes the last item from the List.

Concatenating

```
def languages = ["Java", "Groovy", "JRuby"]
def others = ["Jython", "JavaScript"]
languages += others
===> [Java, Groovy, JRuby, Jython, JavaScript]
languages -= others
===> [Java, Groovy, JRuby]
```

You can easily add two Lists together. You can just as easily subtract them back out again.

Join

```
def languages = ["Java", "Groovy", "JRuby"]
groovy> languages.join()
===> JavaGroovyJRuby
groovy> languages.join(",")
===> Java,Groovy,JRuby
```

The convenience method join() returns a string containing each element in the List. If you pass a string argument into join(), each element will be separated by the string.

Find All

```
def languages = ["Java", "Groovy", "JRuby"]
languages.findAll{ it.startsWith("G") }
===> [Groovy]
```

findAll() allows you to query your List. It returns a new List that contains all the elements that match your criteria.

Max, Min, Sum

```
def scores = [80, 90, 70]
println scores.max()
===> 90
println scores.min()
===> 70
println scores.sum()
===> 240
```

max() returns the highest value in the List. min() returns the lowest. sum() adds up all elements in the List.

Collect

```
def languages = ["Java", "Groovy", "JRuby"]
languages.collect{ it += " is cool"}
===> [Java is cool, Groovy is cool, JRuby is cool]
```

If you want to modify each element in a List, you can use the collect() method. Note that collect() does not modify the original List. It returns a new List.

Flatten

```
def languages = ["Java", "Groovy", "JRuby"]
def others = ["Jython", "JavaScript"]
languages << others
===> [Java, Groovy, JRuby, [Jython, JavaScript]]
languages = languages.flatten()
===> [Java, Groovy, JRuby, Jython, JavaScript]
```

If you have a multidimensional List, flatten() returns a single-dimensional array. Note that flatten() does not modify the original List. It returns a new List.

Spread Operator (*)

```
def params = []
params << "jdbc:mysql://localhost:3306/bookstore_dev?autoreconnect=true"
params << "com.mysql.jdbc.Driver"
params << "username"
params << "password"
def sql = groovy.sql.Sql.newInstance(*params)
```

The spread operator, as the name implies, *spreads* the elements of a List out. In this example, the newInstance method expects four string arguments. *params takes the List and spreads the elements out into each slot of the method arguments.

The spread-dot operator works in the opposite direction. It allows you to concisely iterate over a list, calling the same method on each element:

```
def languages = ["Java", "Groovy", "JRuby"]
println languages*.toUpperCase()
===> [JAVA, GROOVY, JRUBY]
```

3.15 Map Shortcuts

```
def family = [dad:"John", mom:"Jane"]
println family.getClass()
===> java.util.LinkedHashMap
```

Groovy offers a concise syntax for creating Maps. You just put a comma-delimited list of name/value pairs in square brackets to the right of the equals sign, and you have a Map. (Lists offer a similarly easy construct—see Section 3.14, *List Shortcuts*, on page 48.)

Creating an Empty Map

```
def empty = [:]
println empty.size()
===> 0
```

To create an empty Map, simply use the empty set notation with a colon.

Getting an Element

```
def family = [dad:"John", mom:"Jane"]
family.get("dad")
family.dad
===> John
```

You can use the traditional Java get() method to return an element out of the Map. However, Groovy shortens this syntax to make it look as if you were calling the key directly.

If you wanted a more array-like syntax, family['dad'] is yet another way to get an element out of a map.

Gotcha: Why Does .class Work on Everything Except Maps?

```
def family = [dad:"John", mom:"Jane"]
println family.class
===> null
println family.getClass()
===> java.util.LinkedHashMap
```

Since the dot notation is used to get elements out of the Map, calling map.class returns null instead of the class type. Why? Because your Map doesn't contain an element named class. With Maps, you must use the long Java form of the method call—map.getClass(). Of course, getClass() works across all classes, so this might be the safest form of the call to make if you want it to work 100% of the time.

For more information, see the sidebar on page 63.

Adding an Element

```
def family = [dad:"John", mom:"Jane"]
family.put("kid", "Timmy")
family.kid2 = "Susie"
===>  {dad=John, mom=Jane, kid=Timmy, kid2=Susie}
```

You can use the traditional Java put() method to add an element to the Map. Groovy shortens this to the same dotted notation you use for getting elements.

If you prefer a more array-like syntax, family['kid2'] = "Susie" is also valid.

Iterating

```
def family = [dad:"John", mom:"Jane"]

//using the default 'it' variable:
family.each{println it}
===>
dad=John
mom=Jane

//getting the key and value from 'it'
family.each{println "${it.value} is the ${it.key}"}
===>
John is the dad
Jane is the mom
```

```
//using named variables for the key and value
family.each{k,v ->
  println "${v} is the ${k}"
}
===>
John is the dad
Jane is the mom
```

Iterating through a Map is such a common activity that Groovy gives you a convenient way to do it. The first example uses the default name for the iterator variable, it. The next example uses it.key and it.value to grab the separate parts of the name/value pair. The final example explicitly names the key and value variables k and v, respectively.

Concatenating

```
def family = [dad:"John", mom:"Jane"]
def kids = [kid:"Timmy", kid2:"Susie"]
family += kids
===> {dad=John, kid=Timmy, kid2=Susie, mom=Jane}

kids.each{k,v->
  family.remove("${k}")
}
===> {dad=John, mom=Jane}
```

You can easily add two Maps together. Groovy doesn't offer a shortcut for subtracting one Map from the other, but the syntax is so short that it is a minor oversight at best.

Finding Keys

```
def family = [dad:"John", mom:"Jane"]
family.keySet()
===> [dad, mom]

family.containsKey("dad")
===> true
```

You can use the same strategies for finding keys to a Map in Groovy that you use in Java—keySet() returns a List of all the keys, and containsKey() lets you know whether a key exists.

Finding Values

```
def family = [dad:"John", mom:"Jane"]
family.values()
===> [John, Jane]

family.containsValue("John")
===> true
```

You can use the same strategies for finding Map values in Groovy that you use in Java—values() returns a List of all the values, and containsValue() lets you know whether a value exists.

3.16 Ranges

```
def r = 1..3
println r.class
===> groovy.lang.IntRange

r.each{println it}
===>
1
2
3

r.each{ println "Hi" }
===>
Hi
Hi
Hi

(1..3).each{println "Bye"}
===>
Bye
Bye
Bye
```

Groovy offers a native datatype for Ranges. You can store a range in a variable, or you can create and use them on the fly.

All of the examples here use Integers for the sake of simplicity. But Ranges are far more flexible. They can include any class that implements the Comparable interface and has next() and previous() methods. Consider this quick example of a Range of Dates:

```
def today = new Date()
===> Sat Dec 29 23:59:28 MST 2007
def nextWeek = today + 7
===> Sat Jan 05 23:59:28 MST 2008
(today..nextWeek).each{println it}
===>
Sat Dec 29 23:59:28 MST 2007
Sun Dec 30 23:59:28 MST 2007
Mon Dec 31 23:59:28 MST 2007
Tue Jan 01 23:59:28 MST 2008
Wed Jan 02 23:59:28 MST 2008
Thu Jan 03 23:59:28 MST 2008
Fri Jan 04 23:59:28 MST 2008
Sat Jan 05 23:59:28 MST 2008
```

Size, From, To

```
def r = 1..3
r.size()
===> 3
r.from
===> 1
r.to
===> 3
```

We can interrogate ranges about their size, starting point, and ending point.

For

```
for(i in 1..3){ println "Attempt ${i}" }
===>
Attempt 1
Attempt 2
Attempt 3

(1..3).each{ println "Attempt ${it}" }
===>
Attempt 1
Attempt 2
Attempt 3
```

Ranges are commonly used in for loops, although calling each directly on the Range is a bit more concise.

Contains

```
def r = 1..3
r.contains(1) && r.contains(3)
===> true
r.contains(2)
===> true
r.contains(12)
===> false
```

Ranges can tell you whether an arbitrary value falls within the range. Both the start and end points are included in the range.

Reverse

```
r.reverse()
===> [3, 2, 1]
```

If you need to iterate backward through a Range, there is a convenient reverse() method.

3.17 Closures and Blocks

```
def hi = { println "Hi"}
hi()
===> Hi
```

In its simplest form, a groovy.lang.Closure is a free-standing, named block of code. It is behavior that doesn't have a surrounding class.

Really, a closure is not a completely foreign concept. We have code blocks in Java (if, for, while, try, catch, and so on), just not *named* code blocks. Groovy adds this tiny semantic difference and leverages it to a great extent. (For a real-world example of closures in action, see Section 11.8, *Understanding Controllers and Views*, on page 212.)

I humbly offer my apologies if you don't think this is a closure in the strictest academic sense[7] of the word. I'm also going to consciously avoid using phrases such as "lambda-style functional programming."[8] I'm not being coy—the simple fact of the matter is that the implementing class is named Closure.

Accepting Parameters

```
def hello = { println "Hi ${it}" }
hello("John")
hello "John"
===> Hi John
```

The familiar anonymous it parameter discussed in Section 3.14, *List Shortcuts*, on page 48 and Section 3.15, *Map Shortcuts*, on page 52 comes into play here as well. Notice that you can leave off the parentheses when calling a closure just as you would if you were calling a method. (See Section 3.3, *Optional Parentheses*, on page 34 for more information.)

Here's a slightly more advanced example of closures in action. Notice how the it parameter is used in both the each and the convertToCelsius closures.

```
def convertToCelsius = {
  return (5.0/9.0) * (it.toFloat() - 32.0)
}

[0, 32, 70, 100].each{
  println "${it} degrees fahrenheit in celsius: ${convertToCelsius(it)}"
}
```

---

7. http://en.wikipedia.org/wiki/Closure_\%28computer_science\%29
8. http://en.wikipedia.org/wiki/Functional_programming

```
===>
0    degrees fahrenheit in celsius: -17.7777777792
32   degrees fahrenheit in celsius: 0.0
70   degrees fahrenheit in celsius: 21.1111111128
100  degrees fahrenheit in celsius: 37.7777777808
```

Named Parameters

```
def calculateTax = { taxRate, amount ->
  return amount + (taxRate * amount)
}

println "Total cost: ${calculateTax(0.055, 100)}"
===> Total cost: 105.500
```

Although the anonymous it parameter is very convenient when writing quick-and-dirty ad hoc scripts, naming your parameters will help the readability and maintainability of your code in the long run. If your closure expects more than one parameter, you really don't have a choice but to name them.

Currying Parameters

```
def calculateTax = { taxRate, amount ->
  return amount + (taxRate * amount)
}

def tax = calculateTax.curry(0.1)
[10,20,30].each{
  println "Total cost: ${tax(it)}"
}
===>
Total cost: 11.0
Total cost: 22.0
Total cost: 33.0
```

When you instantiate a closure, you can preload values into the parameters by using the curry method. In this example, hard-coding a default value for taxRate would significantly reduce the closure's reusability. On the other hand, having to pass in the same tax rate each time you call the closure is needlessly repetitive and verbose. Currying the taxRate strikes just the right balance.

You can curry as many parameters as you like. The first curry call fills in the leftmost parameter. Each subsequent call fills in the next parameter to the right.

Chapter 4

Java and Groovy Integration

One of the biggest selling points of Groovy is its seamless integration with Java. In this chapter, we'll explore this integration in various ways. We'll look at using plain old Groovy objects (POGOs) as drop-in replacements for plain old Java objects (POJOs). We'll call Groovy code from Java and Java code from Groovy. And finally we'll explore how to use Ant to compile our entire project, including a healthy combination of Groovy and Java classes.

4.1 GroovyBeans (aka POGOs)

```
package org.davisworld.bookstore

class Book{
  String title
  String author
  Integer pages
}
```

As we saw in Section 1.1, *Groovy, the Way Java Should Be*, on page 5, this is all there is to a POGO. Groovy boils JavaBeans down to their pure essence.

Packaging

The first thing you'll notice in this example is the packaging. You'll probably never need to package ad hoc Groovy scripts, but Groovy classes are packaged in the same way as Java classes. (See Chapter 5, *Groovy from the Command Line*, on page 77 for more on writing Groovy scripts.) The only thing that might seem strange to a Java developer's eye is the missing semicolon. (As we discussed in Section 3.2, *Optional Semicolons*, on page 32, you can add it back in if you'd like.)

Public Classes, Private Attributes, Public Methods

```groovy
// in Groovy:
class Book{
  String title

  String toString(){
    return title
  }
}
```

```java
// in Java:
public class Book{
  private String title;

  public String toString(){
    return title;
  }
}
```

Classes in Groovy are implicitly public if you don't provide an access modifier (public, private, or protected). In Java, classes are package-private if you don't say otherwise. This can be a serious "gotcha" if you aren't paying attention when you move back and forth between the two languages. (See the sidebar on the facing page for more on this.)

Attributes in Groovy are implicitly private if you don't provide an access modifier. You can prove this through a little bit of introspection:

```
println Book.getDeclaredField("title")
===> private java.lang.String Book.title
```

Methods in Groovy are public by default. Here's the proof:

```
println Book.getDeclaredMethod("toString")
===> public java.lang.String Book.toString()
```

So, what do Groovy developers have against package-private access? Nothing, really. Their goal was to allow classes to do the right thing by default, and package-private access was an unfortunate bit of collateral damage.

Think about the last major Java project you worked on for a minute. How many public POJOs did you have with private attributes? You can probably safely invoke the "80/20 rule" here, but if I pressed you, it'd most likely end up being 90% or greater. Public classes with private attributes are the overwhelming majority of the Java code written, and Groovy's intelligent defaults reflect this business reality.

> ### Gotcha: No Package-Private Visibility
>
> In Java, if you leave the access modifier off a class, attribute, or method, it means that other classes in the same package or direct subclasses in another package can access them directly. This is called package-private access.* In Groovy, classes without an access modifier are considered public. Attributes without an access modifier are considered private. Methods without an access modifier are public. Although this shortcut is arguably more useful for mainstream usage, it represents one of the few cases where Java semantics differ from Groovy semantics.
>
> There is no way to give classes, attributes, or methods package-private visibility in Groovy. Public, private, and protected elements are all declared in Groovy the same way as they are in Java.
>
> ---
> *. http://java.sun.com/docs/books/tutorial/java/javaOO/accesscontrol.html

4.2 Autogenerated Getters and Setters

```
class Book{
  String title
}

Book book = new Book()
book.setTitle("Groovy Recipes")

println book.getTitle()
===> Groovy Recipes
```

Although the absence of the oh-so-obvious public and private modifiers cut down the class size a bit, it is the automatic generation of the getters and setters that makes the real difference. Every attribute in a POGO gets a matching set by default.

Think once again back to your last Java project. Did you lovingly hand-craft each getter and setter, or did you let your IDE generate the boilerplate code?

If this code is rote and uninteresting, letting the Groovy compiler, instead of your IDE, generate it for you dramatically reduces the visual clutter in your project. And if, by chance, you are overriding the default behavior of a getter or a setter, see how your eye is immediately drawn to the exception to the rule:

```
class Book{
  String title
  String author
  Integer pages

  String getTitle(){
    return title.toUpperCase()
  }
}
```

Getter and Setter Shortcut Syntax

```
class Book{
  String title
}

Book book = new Book()
book.title = "Groovy Recipes"
//book.setTitle("Groovy Recipes")

println book.title
//println book.getTitle()
===> Groovy Recipes
```

Yet another way Groovy cuts down on visual clutter is the syntactic shortcut it allows when dealing with class attributes. book.title is calling book.getTitle() behind the scenes. This is an attempt to make it feel more natural—it seems to be dealing with the Book's title directly, rather than calling the getTitle() method on the Book class that returns a String value. (For more information, see the sidebar on the next page.)

The legacy Java getter and setter syntax is still perfectly valid in Groovy.

Suppressing Getter/Setter Generation

```
class Book2{
  private String title
}

println Book2.getDeclaredField("title")
===> private java.lang.String Book2.title

println Book2.methods.each{println it}; "DONE"
// neither getTitle() nor setTitle() should appear in the list
```

Explicitly flagging a field as private in Groovy suppresses the creation of the corresponding getter and setter methods. This little gem is quite helpful if you want the field to be truly hidden from Java classes.

Groovy Syntax Shortcuts

As demonstrated in Section 4.2, *Getter and Setter Shortcut Syntax*, on the facing page, book.getTitle() can be shortened to book.title. Although this getter/setter shortcut is the default behavior in Groovy, there are numerous places in the language where it is selectively overridden to mean something completely different.

In Section 3.15, *Map Shortcuts*, on page 52, a call like book.title on a hashmap is a shortcut for book.get("title"). In Chapter 7, *Parsing XML*, on page 107, that same call is a quick way to parse an XML snippet such as <book><title>Groovy Recipes</title></book>. In Section 10.8, *Calling Methods That Don't Exist (invokeMethod)*, on page 185, you'll learn how to take that call and do pretty much whatever you'd like with it.

I don't consider this to be a gotcha; in fact, I consider it a powerful language feature. But it can catch you off-guard if you aren't expecting it.

But what about visibility to other Groovy classes? Well, this code snippet should make it abundantly clear that the field is still accessible despite the lack of getter and setter methods:

```
def b2 = new Book2()
b2.title = "Groovy Recipes"
println b2.title
===> Groovy Recipes
```

Groovy has some issues with privacy—in a nutshell, it ignores the private modifier. (Yeah, that's a pretty big issue. See the sidebar on page 70 for more information.)

If you want to protect a private field from accidental modification in Groovy, you can add a pair of do-nothing getters and setters. Flagging the methods as private will prevent them from cluttering up the public API.

```
class Book3{
  private String title
  private String getTitle(){}
  private void setTitle(title){}
}
```

```
def b3 = new Book3()
b3.title = "Groovy Recipes"
println b3.title
===> null
```

It is important that your dummy getters and setters don't modify the value of the private field. Since Groovy ignores the private modifier on the methods, you are actually invoking them when you call b3.title.

Although creating do-nothing getters and setters will protect your private field from casual users, adding an @ prefix to the field name allows you to access any field directly—public, private, or protected. The @ bypasses any getters and setters that might be in place, so at the end of the day there is really no way to prevent a determined user from breaking encapsulation and mucking around with your private bits directly. (For more information, see Section 10.6, *Creating a Field Pointer*, on page 184.)

```
class Book3{
  private String title
  private String getTitle(){}
  private void setTitle(title){}
}

def b3 = new Book3()
b3.@title = "Groovy Recipes"
println b3.@title
===> Groovy Recipes
```

4.3 getProperty and setProperty

```
class Book{
  String title
}

Book book = new Book()
book.setProperty("title", "Groovy Recipes")
//book.title = "Groovy Recipes"
//book.setTitle("Groovy Recipes")

println book.getProperty("title")
//println book.title
//println book.getTitle()
===> Groovy Recipes
```

This example shows a third way of setting and getting properties on a POGO—book.getProperty() and book.setProperty(). In traditional Java, calling book.getTitle() is second nature. As we discussed in Section 4.2,

Getter and Setter Shortcut Syntax, on page 62, Groovy allows you to shorten book.getTitle() to book.title. But what if you want a more generic way to deal with the fields of a class?

Groovy borrows a trick from java.lang.System in providing a generic way to access the properties of a class. As discussed in Section 5.8, *Getting System Properties*, on page 83, you can't make a method call such as System.getJavaVersion(). You must ask for System properties in a more generic way—System.getPropery("java.version"). To get a list of all properties, you ask for System.getProperties(). These generic methods are now available on every class, courtesy of the groovy.lang.GroovyObject interface.

Yes, you could always do this sort of thing with the java.lang.reflect package, but Groovy makes the syntax easy to work with. Once you start dealing with metaprogramming on a more regular basis, this way of interacting with classes will become as natural as book.getTitle() or book.title. For more on this, see Section 10.2, *Discovering the Fields of a Class*, on page 175.

Property Access with GStrings

```
class Book{
  String title
}

def b = new Book()
def prop = "title"
def value = "Groovy Recipes"
b."${prop}" = value
println b."${prop}"
===> Groovy Recipes
```

As nice as the getProperty and setProperty methods are, there is an even "groovier" way to generically deal with fields. You can pass the name of the field into a GString for maximum flexibility. (For more on GStrings, see Section 3.13, *GStrings*, on page 47.)

4.4 Making Attributes Read-Only

```
class Book{
  final String title

  Book(title){
    this.title = title
  }
}
```

```
Book book = new Book()
book.title = "Groovy Recipes"
===>
ERROR groovy.lang.ReadOnlyPropertyException:
Cannot set readonly property: title for class: Book

Book book2 = new Book("GIS for Web Developers")
println book2.title
===>
GIS for Web Developers
```

The final modifier works the same way in both Groovy and Java. Specifically, it means that the attribute can be set only when the class is instantiated. If you try to modify the attribute after the fact, a groovy.lang.ReadOnlyPropertyException is thrown.

4.5 Constructor Shortcut Syntax

```
class Book{
  String title
  String author
  Integer pages
}

Book book1 = new Book(title:"Groovy Recipes", author:"Scott Davis", pages:250)
Book book2 = new Book(pages:230, author:"Scott Davis",
                  title:"GIS for Web Developers")
Book book3 = new Book(title:"Google Maps API")
Book book4 = new Book()
```

Groovy offers constructor convenience like nothing you've ever seen in Java. By supporting named arguments and a variable-length argument list, you can instantiate your class in any way you see fit. book1 and book2 demonstrate that since the variables are named, you can supply them in any order. book3 demonstrates the vararg part of the equation: in this case, you just pass in the title. book4 demonstrates that none of the Groovy convenience methods interferes with the default Java constructor.

What's especially neat about this constructor shortcut is that it is available on pure Java classes as well. The constructor behavior is added at runtime, so it works for either Groovy or Java classes. For a real-world demonstration of this, see Section 4.9, *Calling Java from Groovy*, on page 71.

4.6 Optional Parameters/Default Values

```
class Payment{
  BigDecimal amount
  String type

  public Payment(BigDecimal amount, String type="cash"){
    this.amount = amount
    this.type = type
  }

  String toString(){
    return "${amount} ${type}"
  }
}

def pmt1 = new Payment(10.50, "cash")
println pmt1
//===> 10.50 cash

def pmt2 = new Payment(12.75)
println pmt2
//===> 12.75 cash

def pmt3 = new Payment(15.99, "credit")
println pmt3
//===> 15.99 credit
```

In this example, type defaults to "cash" unless you explicitly provide
another value. This streamlines the development process by not requiring you to maintain two separate overloaded constructors—one that
accepts just an amount and a second one that accepts an amount and
a type. The really nice thing about optional parameters is that they are
available on any type of method. Consider the following method that
streamlines the purchase of a movie ticket:

```
class Ticket{
  static String buy(Integer quantity=1, String ticketType="adult"){
    return "${quantity} x ${ticketType}"
  }
}

println Ticket.buy()
println Ticket.buy()
println Ticket.buy(2)
println Ticket.buy(4, "child")
===>
1 x adult
1 x adult
2 x adult
4 x child
```

In this example, a single method offers a great deal of flexibility. If you call it without parameters, it uses intelligent defaults for everything. The next most likely scenario (in theory) is two people out on a date— the code allows you to override the quantity while still defaulting the ticketType to "adult."

In the Payment example, the amount has no default value. You are required to provide it every time you create a new Payment. The type, on the other hand, defaults to "cash" if not provided. Optional parameters must always come after all the required parameters. Optional parameters should also be ordered by importance—the most likely parameter to change should come first in the list, followed by the next most likely, and so on, down to the least likely to be overridden of all.

```
static String buy(Integer quantity=1, String ticketType="adult",
  BigDecimal discount=0.0)

//won't compile
Ticket.buy(0.15)

//will compile
Ticket.buy(1, "adult", 0.15)
```

Given the order of the parameters in the new buy() method, there is no way you can request a 15% discount on one adult ticket without specifying all three values. The cascading order of importance in the optionals list says that you can safely ignore parameters to the right of you, but you must specify parameters to the left of you.

4.7 Private Methods

```
class Book{
  String title

  private String getTitle(){
    return title
  }
  private void setTitle(String title){
    this.title = title
  }

  private void poke(){
    println "Ouch!"
  }
}

Book book = new Book()
```

```
// notice that Groovy completely ignores the private access modifier
book.title = "Groovy Recipes"
println book.title
===> Groovy Recipes

book.poke()
===> Ouch!
```

Simply put, Groovy pays no attention to the private access modifier for methods. You can call private methods as easily as you can call public ones. (For more on this, see the sidebar on the next page.)

Private methods don't show up in the public interface. This means that poke() doesn't appear when you call Book.methods.each{println it}. The only way you'd know that poke() is available is if you had the source code in front of you.

Java respects the private modifier. When instantiated in Java, you cannot call poke() through normal means.

4.8 Calling Groovy from Java

```
public class BookstoreJava implements Bookstore {
  private Book b;        // written in Groovy
  private Publisher p;   // written in Java

  public Book makeBook() {
    b = new Book();
    b.setAuthor("Scott Davis");
    b.setTitle("Groovy Recipes");
    b.setPages(250);
    return b;
  }

  public Publisher makePublisher() {
    p = new Publisher();
    p.setName("Pragmatic Bookshelf");
    return p;
  }
}
```

You might be squinting at this point, looking for evidence that Book was implemented in Groovy and that Publisher was implemented in Java. *That's the point!* Once a class written in Groovy is compiled, it looks no different from a class written in Java. The autogenerated getters and setters (Section 4.2, *Autogenerated Getters and Setters*, on page 61) are indistinguishable from ones implemented in Java. This makes Groovy a perfect drop-in replacement for your JavaBeans.

Gotcha: Groovy Ignores the Private Modifier

As demonstrated in Section 4.7, *Private Methods*, on page 68, Groovy allows you to call private methods on a class just as easily as public ones. As demonstrated in Section 4.2, *Suppressing Getter/Setter Generation*, on page 62, Groovy allows you to access private fields as if they were public.

The bottom line is that Java respects the private access modifier; Groovy doesn't. Java is the neighbor that knocks on your front door even though it knows where you hide the key. Groovy is the neighbor that lets itself in to borrow a cup of sugar and leaves you a note on the kitchen table. When I first started working with Groovy, this was the (ahem) *feature* that I found most unsettling. At best it seems impolite to ignore the private modifier. At worst, it can be downright dangerous.

Maybe it's Groovy's cavalier attitude toward privacy that made me uncomfortable initially. It's so easy to call a private method that you think, "This *has* to be a bug." You can, of course, bypass the private modifier in Java as well by using the java.lang.reflect package. But calling private methods in Java, for some reason, just seems more circumspect. You have to consciously go out of your way to call a private method in Java. You have to know what you are doing. We are well off the beaten path in Java—there is no mistaking that we are doing something out of the ordinary.

Although the lack of privacy in Groovy still occasionally bothers me intellectually, in practice this really hasn't been much of an issue. Private methods don't show up in the public interface, so usually the only way I know that a private method exists is if I have the source code open in front of me. If I have that level of access to the class, the onus is on me not to hopelessly screw things up. Along those same lines, having access to private methods and fields can actually be quite helpful when staging a class for unit testing, especially if it wasn't written to be easily testable.

Bjarne Stroustrup famously said, "C makes it easy to shoot yourself in the foot; C++ makes it harder, but when you do, it blows your whole leg off." Some might argue that in the case of private methods, Groovy makes it *easier* to blow your whole leg off. My personal take on the issue is a bit more pragmatic: I'd rather have a sharper scalpel and a better-trained surgeon than a duller blade. It's the responsibility of the developer to use this feature wisely.

You get identical behavior using a fraction of the code that you would have to use in a pure Java implementation. The only things required for this code to work are that your Groovy classes be compiled (which we discuss in Section 4.11, *The Groovy Joint Compiler*, on the next page) and that the single Groovy JAR found in $GROOVY_HOME/embeddable is somewhere on your classpath.

4.9 Calling Java from Groovy

```groovy
class BookstoreGroovy implements Bookstore{
  Book b        // written in Groovy
  Publisher p   // written in Java

  Book makeBook(){
    b = new Book(author:"Scott Davis", pages:250, title:"Groovy Recipes")
  }

  Publisher makePublisher(){
    p = new Publisher(name:"Pragmatic Bookshelf")
  }
}
```

In Section 4.8, *Calling Groovy from Java*, on page 69, we saw that Groovy classes look just like Java classes when run from Java. In this example, you can see that Java classes look just like Groovy classes when run from Groovy. Even though Publisher is written in Java, you can still use the cool constructor shortcut (Section 4.5, *Constructor Shortcut Syntax*, on page 66) available to you in Groovy.

4.10 Interfaces in Groovy and Java

```java
// Bookstore.java
public interface Bookstore {
  public Book makeBook();
  public Publisher makePublisher();
}
```

```groovy
// BookstoreGroovy.groovy
class BookstoreGroovy implements Bookstore{...}
```

```java
// BookstoreJava.java
public class BookstoreJava implements Bookstore {...}
```

What you can see here is another example of how well Groovy seamlessly integrates with Java. The Bookstore interface is written in Java. As previously discussed, Book is written in Groovy, and Publisher is written in Java. The interface deals with both classes equally well.

Now take a look at BookstoreGroovy. It is written in Groovy, yet it is able to implement Bookstore (written in Java) as easily as BookstoreJava.

The only things required for this code to work are that your Groovy classes be compiled (which we discuss in Section 4.11, *The Groovy Joint Compiler*) and that the single Groovy JAR found in $GROOVY_HOME/ embeddable is somewhere on your classpath.

4.11 The Groovy Joint Compiler

```
// compile Groovy code
$ groovyc *.groovy

// compile Java code
$ javac *.java

// compile both Groovy and Java code
// using groovyc for the Groovy code and javac for the Java code
$ groovyc * -j -Jclasspath=$GROOVY_HOME/embeddable/groovy-all-1.5.0.jar:.
```

Not surprisingly, groovyc compiles Groovy source into bytecode just as javac compiles Java source. The Groovy compiler, however, adds one more subtle but incredibly useful feature: the ability to jointly compile Java and Groovy code using a single command.

Satisfying Dependencies

To appreciate what groovyc does, let's take a deeper dive into the javac life cycle. Before javac can compile your code, it has to satisfy all the dependencies. For example, let's try to compile the Bookstore interface:

```
$ javac Bookstore.java

// Bookstore.java
public interface Bookstore {
  public Book makeBook();
  public Publisher makePublisher();
}
```

The first thing javac tries to do is find Book and Publisher. Without them, there's no way that Bookstore can be compiled. So, javac searches the CLASSPATH for Book.class and Publisher.class. They might be stored in a JAR or just laying around on their own, but if javac can find them in an already compiled state, it can proceed with the compilation of Bookstore.

If javac can't find Book.class or Publisher.class, then it goes hunting for Book.java and Publisher.java. If it can find the source code, it will compile them on your behalf and then proceed with the compilation of Bookstore. Does that make sense?

OK, so how does Groovy code throw a monkey wrench in the process? Well, unfortunately javac knows how to compile only Java code. Several pluggable compilers are available that can manage many different types of source code—the GNU GCC compiler[1] is a great example. Sadly, javac isn't one of them. If it can't find Book.class or Book.java, it gives up. In our example, if Book is written in Groovy, javac has this to say:

```
$ javac Bookstore.java
Bookstore.java:2: cannot find symbol
symbol  : class Book
location: interface Bookstore
  public Book makeBook();
         ^
1 error
```

In this simple example, the workaround is of the "Hey, Doc, it hurts when I do this" variety. Since javac won't compile your Groovy code for you, try compiling Book.groovy first and *then* compiling Bookstore.java:

```
$ groovyc Book.groovy
$ javac Bookstore.java
$ ls -al

-rw-r--r--  1 sdavis  sdavis  5052 Dec 10 17:03 Book.class
-rw-r--r--@ 1 sdavis  sdavis    60 Dec 10 16:57 Book.groovy
-rw-r--r--  1 sdavis  sdavis   169 Dec 10 17:03 Bookstore.class
-rw-r--r--@ 1 sdavis  sdavis    93 Dec 10 16:56 Bookstore.java
-rw-r--r--  1 sdavis  sdavis   228 Dec 10 17:03 Publisher.class
-rw-r--r--@ 1 sdavis  sdavis    48 Dec 10 16:58 Publisher.java
```

All is well with the world, right? You compiled Book.groovy into bytecode, which allowed javac to compile Bookstore.java with nary a complaint. (Notice that Publisher.java got compiled for free along with Bookstore.java.)

Although manually managing the Groovy/Java dependency chain is feasible for simple projects, it quickly becomes a nightmare if you have Groovy classes that depend on Java classes that depend on Groovy classes—you get the idea.

---

1. http://gcc.gnu.org/

One Command, Two Compilers

```
$ groovyc * -j -Jclasspath=$GROOVY_HOME/embeddable/groovy-all-1.5.0.jar:.
```

Since javac can't be coaxed into compiling Groovy for you, you can look to groovyc for this feature. But make no mistake, *groovyc does not compile Java code.* By passing the -j flag to the compiler, it signals the compiler to use javac for Java code and groovyc for Groovy code. You get all the benefits of dependency resolution across both languages while using each language's native compiler.

The lowercase -j flag turns on joint compilation. You can include multiple uppercase -J flags to pass standard flags to the javac compiler. This example is making sure that javac can find the Groovy JAR by passing in the classpath argument. If you don't have the CLASSPATH environment variable set, you must use the classpath flag. If you don't have the Groovy JAR in the classpath, the Java code won't be able to compile against the Groovy classes.

In this example, you tell javac to generate classes that are compatible with Java 1.4:

```
$ groovyc * -j -Jclasspath=$GROOVY_HOME/embeddable/groovy-all-1.5.0.jar:.
    -Jsource=1.4 -Jtarget=1.4
```

4.12 Compiling Your Project with Ant

```
<taskdef name="groovyc"
         classname="org.codehaus.groovy.ant.Groovyc"
         classpathref="my.classpath"/>

<groovyc
    srcdir="${src}"
    destdir="${dest}"
    classpathref="my.classpath"
    jointCompilationOptions="-j -Jsource=1.4 -Jtarget=1.4" />
```

It's great knowing that you can compile your Groovy code from the command line (Section 4.11, *The Groovy Joint Compiler*, on page 72), but most projects use Ant for this. Luckily, Groovy provides an Ant task for just such an occasion.

To avoid the taskdef step, drop the Groovy JAR from $GROOVY_HOME/ embeddable into the $ANT_HOME/lib directory.

4.13 Compiling Your Project with Maven

`http://mojo.codehaus.org/groovy`

Although Groovy doesn't provide Maven 2.0 support out of the box, the Mojo project does. There is a Maven plug-in that allows you to compile your Groovy code jointly (see Section 4.11, *The Groovy Joint Compiler*, on page 72 for details). There is also a Maven Archetype plug-in that generates a skeleton for your Groovy project.

Chapter 5

Groovy from the Command Line

Java for shell scripting? Yeah, right.

Groovy, on the other hand, has pleasantly surprised me in this respect. Now don't get me wrong—no self-respecting Unix system administrator is going to throw out their self-obfuscating Perl and shell scripts in favor of Groovy. But for me—Java Guy—using a language that I'm intimately familiar with for housekeeping tasks on the server is a perfect fit. I'm not a full-time systems administrator, yet I am consistently faced with chores such as wading through a directory full of Tomcat log files or batch converting a directory full of images from one format to another. Using Groovy for this kind of thing is so natural that I couldn't imagine doing it in any other language.

In this chapter, we'll talk about running uncompiled Groovy scripts from the command prompt and pulling in command-line arguments from the user. You can call other Groovy scripts as easily as you call native operating system commands. Groovy's talent in acting as a glue language is on full display here. Groovy blurs the distinction between native operating system tasks and Java libraries with real aplomb, making administrative tasks—dare I say it?—*almost* enjoyable.

5.1 Running Uncompiled Groovy Scripts

```
groovy hello.groovy
groovy hello
```

The groovy command allows you to run an uncompiled Groovy script. For example, create a file named hello.groovy in the text editor of your choice. Add the following line to it:

```
println "Hello Groovy World"
```

To run your script, type groovy hello.groovy. If you use the .groovy file extension, you can leave the extension off when typing it from the command prompt: groovy hello.

For those of us steeped in enterprise Java development and the accompanying "compile –> JAR –> WAR –> EAR –> deploy" life cycle, it seems almost decadent to think we could actually just save a file and run it. The instant turnaround of "think it –> code it –> run it" gets pretty addictive once you've experienced it.

5.2 Shebanging Groovy

```
#!/usr/bin/env groovy
println "Hello Groovy World"
```

Fans of Unix-like operating systems are familiar with "shebanging" their scripts—a contraction of "hash" and "bang," the first two characters in the first line of the script. Shebanging your script allows you to leave off the command interpreter when typing at the command line. Instead of typing groovy hello to run this script, you can simply type hello.groovy. Since the script is self-aware (that is, it already knows it is a Groovy script), you can even leave off the file extension when naming the file. Typing hello at the command prompt makes it look like a native command.

Shebanging Groovy scripts assumes four things:

- You are on a Unix-like operating system: Linux, Mac OS X, Solaris, and so on (sorry, Windows users, unless you are Cygwin[1] users as well).

- You have made the file executable (chmod a+x hello).

- The current directory (.) is in your PATH. If not, ./hello still isn't too bad.

- The environment variable GROOVY_HOME exists, and GROOVY_HOME/bin is somewhere in your path. You can always hard-code the exact path to the groovy command interpreter at the top of your script, but that prevents you from flipping among various versions of Groovy using the symlink trick discussed in Section 2.1, *Installing Groovy on Unix, Linux, and Mac OS X*, on page 14.

---

1. http://www.cygwin.com/

I have a number of utility scripts that I keep in ~/bin. They are she-banged, chmodded, and already in my path. This means that wherever I am on the filesystem, I can type doSomethingClever, vaguely remembering at some level that I wrote the script in Groovy, but honestly not really caring.

5.3 Accepting Command-Line Arguments

```
if(args){
  println "Hello ${args[0]}"
}
else{
  println "Hello Stranger"
}
```

Remember writing your first HelloWorld Java class? It probably looked something like this:

```
public class HelloWorld{
  public static void main(String[] args){
    if(args != null && args.length > 0){
      System.out.println("Hello " + args[0]);
    }
    else{
      System.out.println("Hello Stranger");
    }
  }
}
```

After a javac HelloWorld.java to compile it, you then ran it by typing java HelloWorld Bub.

Using Groovy, you can boil the same exercise down to its bare essentials. Type the code that started this tip into a file named Hola.groovy. Next type groovy Hola Bub. Since all Groovy scripts are compiled into valid Java bytecode by the groovy command interpreter in memory, you effectively end up with the Java example without having to type all of that additional boilerplate code.

The reason this terse if statement works is thanks to Groovy truth. For more information, see Section 3.10, *Groovy Truth*, on page 44.

Every Groovy script has an implicit argsString array that represents the command-line arguments passed into the script. (You guessed it—this is the args of public static void main(String[] args) fame.) To see the magic args array in action, create a file named cli.groovy, and type the following:

```
args.each{println it}
```

Typing groovy cli this is a test yields the following:

```
$ groovy cli this is a test
===>
this
is
a
test
```

5.4 Running a Shell Command

```
// in Windows:
println "cmd /c dir".execute().text

//in Unix / Linux / Mac OS X:
println "ls -al".execute().text
```

Running a shell command is as simple as calling .execute() on a String. This returns a java.lang.Process. You can use this trick to run full programs or simple command-line tasks. As the code examples demonstrate, the commands inside the String will most likely differ between operating systems. The ls command will work only on Mac OS X, Unix, and Linux systems. The dir command will work only on Windows derivatives.

If you simply call .execute() on a String, the resulting output text is not captured. This might be acceptable for commands such as "rm some-file.txt".execute(). If you want to see the output returned from the shell command, you append .text to the end of .execute().

On Unix-like systems, most shell commands are actually executable programs. Type which ls to see the path to the command. This means that nearly everything you would normally type at the command line can simply be wrapped up in quotes and executed. (One unfortunate exception to this rule is when you are dealing with wildcards. See Section 5.5, *Using Shell Wildcards in Groovy Scripts*, on the next page for more details.) For example, you can run println "ifconfig".execute().text to see the current network settings.

On Windows systems, println "ipconfig /all".execute().text returns similar results. This trick works because ipconfig.exe lives on your path in c:\windows\system32. Unfortunately, many of the most common commands you type at a command prompt in Windows are not executable programs at all. Search as you might, you'll never find a dir.exe or copy.com tucked away in a system directory somewhere. These commands are embedded in cmd.exe.

To execute them, you must type cmd /c. For a list of the embedded commands, type cmd /? at a command prompt. You'll see the following list on Windows XP:

```
DIR
COPY
REN
DEL or ERASE
COLOR
CD or CHDIR
MD or MKDIR
PROMPT
PUSHD
POPD
SET
SETLOCAL
ENDLOCAL
IF
FOR
CALL
SHIFT
GOTO
START
ASSOC
FTYPE
```

Knowing this, many Windows users just prepend cmd /c to all commands they execute in Groovy. Although it's a bit more verbose, it certainly doesn't hurt anything to type "cmd /c ipconfig /all".execute().text.

One last bit of advice for Windows users—don't forget to escape your backslashes in directories: println "cmd /c dir c:\\tmp".execute().text.

5.5 Using Shell Wildcards in Groovy Scripts

```groovy
//in Windows:
println "cmd /c dir *.groovy".execute().text
def c = ["cmd", "/c", "dir *.groovy"].execute().text
println c

//in Unix / Linux / Mac OS X:
def output = ["sh", "-c", "ls -al *.groovy"].execute().text
println output

//sadly, these don't work
println "ls -al *.groovy".execute().text
println "sh -c ls -al *.groovy".execute().text
```

In Section 5.4, *Running a Shell Command*, on the facing page, you learned that some common commands that you type on a Windows machine (dir, copy, and so on) are embedded in the cmd shell. That shell manages wildcard expansion as well. So, asking for all files that end in .groovy is something that the shell expands into a list and then passes on to the dir command.

On Unix-like systems, the shell is responsible for expanding wildcard characters as well. Knowing that, explicitly including the shell in your command makes sense. You can type sh -c "ls -al *.groovy" to get an idea of what we are trying to accomplish.

Unfortunately, the embedded quotes required for this command cause me a bit of heartburn if I try to call execute on a single string. Luckily, we can call execute on a String array as well. The first element in the array is the command, and all the following elements are passed in as arguments. Although this form is a bit more verbose (and admittedly not exactly intuitive at first glance), it *does* work. We get -1 for style points, but +1 for getting the job done....

5.6 Running Multiple Shell Commands at Once

```
//in Windows:
println "cmd /c dir c:\\opt & dir c:\\tmp".execute().text

//in Unix / Linux / Mac OS X:
println "ls /opt & ls /tmp".execute().text
```

You can string together multiple shell commands using the & character. Of course, this has nothing to do with Groovy—this is a feature of the underlying OS. To prove it, try typing the commands surrounded by quotes directly at a command prompt.

5.7 Waiting for a Shell Command to Finish Before Continuing

```
def p = "convert -crop 256x256 full.jpg tile.jpg".execute()
p.waitFor()
println "ls".execute().text
```

If you have a long-running command and want to wait for it to complete before proceeding, you can assign the command to a variable and use the .waitFor() method. This example shows the ImageMagick command convert -crop, which takes a large image and breaks it up into 256-by-256 pixel tiles. You'll want to wait for the command to complete before displaying the directory listing of the current directory to ensure that all the resulting tiles appear.

5.8 Getting System Properties

```
println System.getProperty("java.version")
===> 1.5.0_07

System.properties.each{println it}
===>
java.version=1.5.0_07
java.vm.vendor="Apple Computer, Inc."
os.arch=i386
os.name=Mac OS X
os.version=10.4.10
user.home=/Users/sdavis
...
```

The JVM provides you with a comfortable sandbox, shielding your code from operating system differences. Sun coined the phrase "write once, run anywhere" (WORA) to describe this phenomena, although the old-timers and cynics bend this a bit to "write once, *debug* everywhere."

Almost everything you are doing in this chapter expressly pokes WORA in the eye. You are messing around at the OS level, running commands that will almost certainly break if you try to run them anywhere but the operating system for which they were expressly written. Given that, it's nice to be able to determine programmatically what type of hardware you are running on, what version of the JVM you are using, and so on. The System.properties hashmap allows you to do this type of introspection.

If you already know the name of the variable you are looking for, you can ask for it explicitly; System.getProperty("file.separator"), for example, lets you know whether you should be in a forward-slashy or backward-slashy kind of mood.

On the other hand, you might feel like doing some window shopping instead. Typing System.properties.each{println it} allows you to dump the full list of properties out, one by one. This is a great tool for exposing all the interesting bits of a running system. I usually have this one-liner Groovlet running on each of my production servers so that I can keep an eye on them remotely. (For more on Groovlets, see Section 2.6, *Running Groovy on a Web Server (Groovlets)*, on page 22. For more on keeping your private bits from becoming public bits, see the venerable Tomcat documentation on Security Realms.[2])

---

2. http://tomcat.apache.org/tomcat-6.0-doc/realm-howto.html

Here are various useful system properties as they appear on my MacBook Pro:

```
java.version=1.5.0_07
java.vendor=Apple Computer, Inc.
java.vendor.url=http://apple.com/
java.home=/System/Library/Frameworks/JavaVM.framework/Versions/1.5.0/Home
groovy.home=/opt/groovy
java.class.path=/path/to/some.jar:/path/to/another.jar

file.separator=/
path.separator=:
line.separator=[NOTE: this is the OS-specific newline string.]

os.name=Mac OS X
os.version=10.4.10
os.arch=i386

user.dir=/current/dir/where/you/ran/this/script
java.io.tmpdir=/tmp
user.home=/Users/sdavis
user.name=sdavis
user.country=US
user.language=en
```

file.separator, path.separator, and line.separator

> These, as you already know, are the most common things that vary between Windows and Unix-like operating systems.

user.dir

> This is the current directory (the directory from which the class is being run). Knowing the user.dir is nice if you want to look for directories and files relative to where you are right now.

java.io.tmp

> This is a good place to write short-lived, temporary files. This variable exists on every system, although the exact file path varies. Having a generic dumping ground that is guaranteed to exist on every system is a nice little hidden gem. Just don't expect those files to live beyond the current block of execution.

user.home

> This little fella, like java.io.tmp, is guaranteed to exist on every system, although the exact file path varies. This is a great place to write more permanent data.

Reading in Custom Values from -D or JAVA_OPTS

The System.properties hashmap is good for more than just dealing with the boring old default values that appear on every system. Custom values can be passed into System.properties in a couple of ways. If you have ever used the -D parameter with Ant targets (for example, ant -Dserver.port=9090 deploy), you know they show up in System.properties as well (System.getProperty("server.port")). Values stored in the JAVA_OPTS environment variable also show up in System.properties.

5.9 Getting Environment Variables

```
println System.getenv("JAVA_HOME")
===> /Library/Java/Home

System.env.each{println it}
===>
PWD=/Users/sdavis/groovybook/Book/code/cli
USER=sdavis
LOGNAME=sdavis
HOME=/Users/sdavis
GROOVY_HOME=/opt/groovy
GRAILS_HOME=/opt/grails
JAVA_HOME=/Library/Java/Home
JRE_HOME=/Library/Java/Home
JAVA_OPTS= -Dscript.name=/opt/groovy/bin/groovy
SHELL=/bin/bash
PATH=/opt/local/bin:/usr/local/bin:...
```

Like system properties (as discussed in Section 5.8, *Getting System Properties*, on page 83), environment variables are another rich vein to mine for system-specific information.

If you already know the name of the environment variable you are looking for, you can ask for it explicitly; System.getenv("GROOVY_HOME"), for example, lets you know the directory where Groovy is installed. To iterate through all the environment variables on the system, System.env.each{println it} does the trick.

You may notice some overlap between environment and system variables. For example, System.getProperty("groovy.home") and System. getenv("GROOVY_HOME") both yield the same thing: /opt/groovy. Other times, the specific bit of information you are looking for can be found only in one place or the other. For example, the list of environment variables will likely contain variables such as TOMCAT_HOME, JBOSS_HOME, and ANT_HOME that don't appear in the list of system properties.

Like anything else, having both available to you will be important at different times. Your customization tweaks might come in via environment variables or -D parameters. Those variables might point you toward the user's home directory or an application directory where config files can be found such as server.xml, struts-config.xml, or .bash_profile. The important thing is that you'll be able to manage the whole system, regardless of which specific mechanism is used.

5.10 Evaluating a String

```
def s = "Scott"
def cmdName = "size"
evaluate("println s.${cmdName}()")
===> 5

cmdName = "toUpperCase"
evaluate "println s.${cmdName}()"
===> SCOTT
```

In Section 5.4, *Running a Shell Command*, on page 80, we discussed how to call execute on an arbitrary string. evaluate works slightly differently.

Instead of running a shell command, evaluate allows you to dynamically execute a random string as Groovy code. The previous examples were dynamically calling two methods on a String—size() and toUpperCase(). (Did you notice the optional parentheses in the second example?) This leads to some interesting capabilities, such as being able to iterate over all methods on an object and call them:

```
//NOTE: This is pseudocode -- it won't actually run
def s = "Scott"
s.class.methods.each{cmdName ->
  evaluate("s.${cmdName}()")
}
```

Although this example won't work as written—it does not take into account the arguments that some of the String methods require such as s.substring(2,4)—it shows the potential value of evaluating Groovy code on the fly. It also quite nicely illustrates the risks. If you blindly accept commands from an end user and execute them on the fly, you should be prepared for the script kiddie who sends you rm -Rf /. For a working example of evaluating methods on the fly, see Section 10.4, *Discovering the Methods of a Class*, on page 180.

5.11 Calling Another Groovy Script

```
// hello.groovy
println "Howdy"
```

```
// goodbye.groovy
hello.main()
println "Goodbye"
```

You probably call one Java class from inside another Java class all the time. If the two classes are in the same package, you can call one from the other directly: AnotherClass.doSomething();. If they live in separate packages, you need to import the other package or fully qualify the class: com.elsewhere.AnotherClass.doSomething();. Calling one Groovy script from another works in fundamentally the same way. As long as you remember that Groovy code gets compiled to bytecode on the fly, you'll never go wrong.

In the previous example, hello.groovy gets compiled into the following equivalent Java code:

```
public class hello{
  public static void main(String[] args){
    System.out.println("Howdy");
  }
}
```

The lowercase class name might look strange, but Groovy simply uses the filename as the class name. (Sound familiar?) Script content that isn't explicitly wrapped in a function/closure/whatever is that script's public static void main(String[] args). Two scripts living in the same directory are effectively in the same package. So, calling any script in the same directory as you're in is as simple as calling the static main method on the class.

Calling Another Script with Parameters

```
//hello2.groovy
if(args){
  println "Hello ${args[0]}"
  if(args.size() > 1){
    println "...and your little dog, too: ${args[1]}"
  }
}
```

```
//goodbye2.groovy
hello2.main()
hello2.main("Glenda")
hello2.main("Dorothy", "Toto")
println "Goodbye"
```

Since the script body is effectively the public static void main(String[] args) method, it only follows that you are able to pass in parameters via the provided string array.

Calling Methods in Another Script

```
//hello3.groovy
if(args){
  println "Hello ${args[0]}"
  if(args.size() > 1){
    println "...and your little dog, too: ${args[1]}"
  }
}

def sayHola(){
        println "Hola"
}

//goodbye3.groovy
hello3.main()
hello3.main("Glenda")
hello3.main("Dorothy", "Toto")
println "Goodbye"

h = new hello3()
h.sayHola()
```

If the other script has static methods (such as main), you can call them statically. If the other script defines instance methods, you must instantiate the script before you can call them.

Calling Another Script in a Different Directory

```
evaluate(new File("/some/other/dir/hello.groovy"))
```

Our friend evaluate comes back for another visit. (See Section 5.10, *Evaluating a String*, on page 86 for an alternate use of evaluate.) This time you are evaluating a file instead of an arbitrary string. This effectively calls the main method of the other file.

If you are trying to do anything more complicated with script-to-script calls than what we've already discussed, my recommendation is to compile your scripts to bytecode, place them in the package of your choice, JAR them up, and call them as you would any other Java class.

5.12   Groovy on the Fly (groovy -e)

```
$ groovy -e "println System.properties['java.class.path']"
===>
/opt/groovy/lib/groovy-1.1-beta-2.jar:/System/Library/Frameworks
/JavaVM.framework/Versions/1.5.0/Classes/.compatibility/14compatibility.jar
```

Groovy makes it easy to run code quickly. You can save a file and run it immediately. You can open up a quick Groovy shell or Groovy console to work with the language interactively. But sometimes running a single line of Groovy at the command line is all you need. The -e flag tells Groovy to *evaluate* the string you just passed in.

For example, let's say you are picking up a strange JAR on your classpath. You can type echo $CLASSPATH on a Unix-like system to see if the environment variable is the culprit. (set on a Windows system will give you similar results.) If the classpath comes up empty, there are many other places those pesky JARs can sneak in. Look in $JAVA_HOME/lib, $JAVA_HOME/lib/ext, and $GROOVY_HOME/lib to see if any strangers are lurking around. The previous example will show you exactly what the JRE sees—it is up to you to hunt down the intruders from there.

5.13   Including JARs at the Command Line

```
$ groovy -classpath ~/lib/derbyclient.jar:~/lib/jdom.jar:. db2xml.groovy
```

If you have a script that depends on other libraries, you can pass groovy a -classpath switch with a list of JARs. This is, of course, no different from running java from the command line. To run our fictional db2xml.groovy script, it's not surprising that the script needs access to both a database driver and an XML library.

Automatically Including JARs in the .groovy/lib Directory

```
//on Windows:
mkdir C:\Documents and Settings\UserName\.groovy\lib

//on Unix, Linux, and Mac OS X:
mkdir ~/.groovy/lib

// uncomment the following line in
// $GROOVY_HOME/conf/groovy-starter.conf
# load user specific libraries
load !{user.home}/.groovy/lib/*.jar
```

You'll soon grow tired of having to type commonly used JARs (such as JDBC drivers) on the command line each time. If you create a .groovy/lib directory in your home directory (don't forget the leading dot), any JARs found in this directory will be automatically included in the CLASSPATH when you run Groovy from the command prompt. The .groovy/lib directory is disabled by default; be sure to enable it in $GROOVY_HOME/conf/groovy-starter.conf.

Chapter 6

File Tricks

Groovy offers many shortcuts for dealing with files and directories. Listing files, copying files, renaming files, deleting files—Groovy brings welcome help for all these mundane tasks. The fact that Groovy adds new
methods directly to the standard JDK classes such as java.io.File make
these new features feel like a natural part of the language.

The stalwart Java build tool Ant makes a cameo appearance in this
chapter as well. Ant goes far beyond the standard Java I/O library
capabilities, adding support for related functionality such as batch
operations and ZIP files. Even though Ant is written in Java, the interface most developers are familiar with is the ubiquitous build.xml file.
Groovy's native support for XML is covered extensively in Chapter 7,
Parsing XML, on page 107 and Chapter 8, *Writing XML*, on page 127. In
this chapter, you'll see a great example of this in action with AntBuilder—
all the power of Ant, none of the XML. It's pure code all the way; you'll
never look at build files the same way again.

6.1 Listing All Files in a Directory

```
new File(".").eachFile{file ->
  println file
}

//prints both files and directories
===>
./error.jsp
./GroovyLogo.zip
./index.jsp
./META-INF
./result.jsp
./WEB-INF
```

The eachFile method that Groovy adds to the standard java.io.File makes short work of displaying a directory listing. In this case, you're looking at the current directory ("."). You can, of course, pass in a fully qualified directory name as well: new File("/opt/tomcat/webapps/myapp").

To give you an idea of the keystrokes Groovy saves you, here is the corresponding code in Java:

```
import java.io.File;

public class DirList {
  public static void main(String[] args) {
    File dir = new File(".");
    File[] files = dir.listFiles();
    for (int i = 0; i < files.length; i++) {
      File file = files[i];
      System.out.println(file);
    }
  }
}
```

Again, you should note that Groovy augments the java.io.File object that comes with Java. This means that all the standard JDK methods are available for use as well as the new Groovy ones. The eachFile method is added to the class, as discussed in Section 10.11, *Adding Methods to a Class Dynamically (ExpandoMetaClass)*, on page 190. To see all the methods added to java.io.File, refer to the GDK documentation.[1]

Command-Line Input

```
$ groovy list /some/other/dir

//list.groovy:
new File(args[0]).eachFile{file ->
  println file
}
```

For a more flexible version of this script, you can borrow the trick discussed in Section 5.3, *Accepting Command-Line Arguments*, on page 79. Assuming that this script is saved in a file named list.groovy, this example gives you the flexibility to pass in any directory name.

Listing Only Directories

```
new File(".").eachDir{dir ->
  println dir
}
```

---

1. http://groovy.codehaus.org/groovy-jdk.html

```
===>
./META-INF
./WEB-INF
```

To limit your output to directories, you use File.eachDir. You can also use File.eachDirRecurse to traverse the entire directory tree:

```
new File(".").eachDirRecurse{dir ->
  println dir
}
```

```
===>
./META-INF
./WEB-INF
./WEB-INF/classes
./WEB-INF/classes/org
./WEB-INF/classes/org/davisworld
./WEB-INF/lib
```

Listing Only Files

```
new File(".").eachFile{file ->
  if(file.isFile()){
    println file
  }
}
```

```
===>
./error.jsp
./GroovyLogo.zip
./index.jsp
./result.jsp
```

At the beginning of this section, we saw that File.eachFile returns both files and directories. (Don't blame Groovy—this mirrors the standard JDK behavior of File.listFiles.) Luckily, you can use another standard JDK method to filter your output: File.isFile.

Groovy also offers a File.eachFileRecurse method that allows you to see all files in the directory tree:

```
new File(".").eachFileRecurse{file ->
  if(file.isFile()){
    println file
  }
}
```

```
===>
./error.jsp
./GroovyLogo.zip
./index.jsp
./result.jsp
```

```
./META-INF/MANIFEST.MF
./WEB-INF/web.xml
./WEB-INF/classes/org/davisworld/MyServlet.class
./WEB-INF/lib/groovy.jar
```

Listing Specific Files in a Directory

```
new File(".").eachFile{file ->
  if(file.name.endsWith(".jsp")){
    println file
  }
}
```

```
===>
./error.jsp
./index.jsp
./result.jsp
```

The if statement is a perfect example of using Groovy and Java together. file.name is the Groovy equivalent of file.getName(), as discussed in Section 4.2, *Getter and Setter Shortcut Syntax*, on page 62. file.name returns a String, which allows you to use the standard JDK endsWith() method.

If you're a fan of regular expressions, Groovy offers a File.eachFileMatch method:

```
new File(".").eachFileMatch(~/.*\.jsp/){file ->
  println file
}
```

File.eachFileMatch technically accepts any class with a method boolean isCase(String s). This means you could expand the example to include a JspFilter class:

```
class JspFilter {
  boolean isCase(String filename) {
    return filename.endsWith(".jsp")
  }
}
```

```
new File(".").eachFileMatch(new JspFilter()){file ->
  println file
}
```

Unfortunately, File.eachFileMatch passes File.getName() to the filter class, not File.getAbsolutePath(). In other words, the filter sees MyServlet.class, not ./WEB-INF/classes/davisworld/MyServlet.class. This means that in order to do any sophisticated filtering on the list (for example, listing only those files bigger than a certain size), you should use File.eachFile or File.eachFileRecurse with your own if statement rather than relying on File.eachFileMatch.

```
//list files greater than 500kb
new File(".").eachFile{file ->
  if(file.size() > (500 * 1024)){
    println file
  }
}

===>
./GroovyLogo.zip
```

6.2 Reading the Contents of a File

```
new File("x.txt").eachLine{line->
  println line
}
```

Just as you can walk through each file in a directory, you can also easily walk through each line of a file using File.eachLine. For binary files, there is also File.eachByte.

Section 8.14, *Converting CSV to XML*, on page 139 demonstrates a slightly more sophisticated version of File.eachLine. In the example, a comma-separated value (CSV) file is walked through line by line using File.splitEachLine.

Reading the Contents of a File into a String Variable

```
String body = new File("x.txt").text
```

It's pretty convenient to be able to read in the entire contents of a file using a single method: File.getText(). This trick will prove to be convenient in later sections such as Section 6.4, *Copying Files*, on page 99 and Section 6.3, *Appending Data to an Existing File*, on page 98.

For binary files, Groovy offers an alternate method, File.readBytes, which returns the entire contents as a byte[].

Reading the Contents of a File into an ArrayList

```
List lines = new File("x.txt").readLines()
```

File.readLines returns the contents of the file as an ArrayList: one element per line in the file. This provides the convenience of having the entire file in memory (like File.getText()), while still allowing you to iterate through it line by line (like File.eachLine).

Quick-and-Dirty File Content Analysis

```
// juliet.txt
O Romeo, Romeo! wherefore art thou Romeo?
Deny thy father and refuse thy name;
Or, if thou wilt not, be but sworn my love,
And I'll no longer be a Capulet.

// FileStats.groovy
File file = new File("juliet.txt")
List lines = file.readLines()
println "Number of lines: ${lines.size()}"
int wordCount = 0
file.splitEachLine(" "){words ->
  println words.size()
  wordCount += words.size()
}
println "Number of words: ${wordCount}"

===>
Number of lines: 4
7
7
10
7
Number of words: 31
```

Using the few convenience methods on File that we've discussed in this section, you can easily return some metadata such as line and word count. In this case, I chose a quick snippet from *Romeo and Juliet*.[2] As programmers, it's not too much of a reach to imagine a Groovy script that could recurse through a directory, looking only at .java files, and return a basic line count/file count for your project, is it?

6.3 Writing Text to a File

```
File file = new File("hello.txt")
file.write("Hello World\n")
println file.text
===>
Hello World

println file.readLines().size()
===>
1
```

---

2. http://www.gutenberg.org/dirs/etext98/2ws1610.txt

The convenience of a single File.write method in Groovy is pretty breath-taking. Contrast the four lines of Groovy code with the forty-plus lines of corresponding Java code:

```java
import java.io.*;

public class NewFile {
  public static void main(String[] args) {
    File file = new File("hello.txt");
    PrintWriter pw = null;
    try {
      pw = new PrintWriter(new BufferedWriter(new FileWriter(file)));
      pw.println("Hello World");
    } catch (IOException e) {
      e.printStackTrace();
    }
    finally{
      pw.flush();
      pw.close();
    }

    BufferedReader br = null;
    int lineCount = 0;
    try {
      br = new BufferedReader(new FileReader(file));
      String line = null;
      while((line = br.readLine()) != null){
        System.out.println(line);
        lineCount++;
      }
    } catch (FileNotFoundException e) {
      e.printStackTrace();
    } catch (IOException e) {
      e.printStackTrace();
    }
    finally{
      try {
        br.close();
      } catch (IOException e) {
        e.printStackTrace();
      }
    }
    System.out.println(lineCount);
  }
}
```

The File.write method is destructive: the contents of the file are overwritten with the new data. The ability to write an entire file in a single line of code is used to great effect in Section 6.4, *Copying Files*, on page 99.

Appending Data to an Existing File

```
File file = new File("hello.txt")
println "${file.size()} lines"
===> 1 lines
file.append("How's it going?\n")
file << "I'm fine, thanks.\n"
println "${file.size()} lines"
===> 3 lines
```

While File.write is a destructive call, File.append leaves the existing content in place, adding the new text to the end of the file.

Did you notice the operator overloading in action? The << operator is equivalent to the append() method call. (See Section 3.7, *Operator Overloading*, on page 40 for more information.)

Merging Several Text Files

```
? ls -al
drwxr-xr-x  8 sdavis   sdavis    272 Dec  2 13:02 .
drwxr-xr-x  4 sdavis   sdavis    136 Dec  2 12:53 ..
-rw-r--r--@ 1 sdavis   sdavis    759 Nov 29 01:04 access.2007-11-28.log
-rw-r--r--@ 1 sdavis   sdavis    823 Nov 30 01:01 access.2007-11-29.log
-rw-r--r--@ 1 sdavis   sdavis    654 Dec  1 01:02 access.2007-11-30.log
-rw-r--r--@ 1 sdavis   sdavis    233 Dec  2 13:04 merge.groovy
drwxr-xr-x  2 sdavis   sdavis     68 Dec  2 12:59 summary
```

```
// merge.groovy
File logDir = new File(".")
File mergedFile = new File("summary/merged.log")
mergedFile.write("") //empty out the existing file
logDir.eachFile{file ->
  if(file.isFile() && file.name.endsWith(".log")){
    mergedFile << file.text
  }
}
```

At the end of each month, I like rolling up my web server's daily traffic files into a monthly summary. With a mere eight lines of code, I can do this with ease. I create a file in the summary directory named merged.log. If the file already exists, a quick mergedFile.write("") ensures that it is emptied out of any data from the previous run. I then walk through each item in the current directory, limiting my focus to files that end with .log. (The file.isFile check makes sure I don't accidentally include a directory name that ends with .log.) mergedFile.append(file.text) takes the file contents of the current file and appends it to mergedFile.

6.4 Copying Files

```
def src = new File("src.txt")
new File("dest.txt").write(src.text)
```

Combining the tricks from Section 6.2, *Reading the Contents of a File*, on page 95 and Section 6.3, *Writing Text to a File*, on page 96, you can see how easy it is to quickly write the text of one file to another.

You might think it's odd that Groovy doesn't provide a simple copy method to do this on your behalf. I wish I had a better response than "Uh, I agree." At any rate, there are several other ways to copy files using Groovy that are worth looking into. And thanks to the dynamic nature of Groovy, at the end of this section I'll show you how to fix this interesting API omission. (You might also take a look at Section 6.5, *Using AntBuilder to Copy a File*, on the following page for yet *another* way to copy files.)

Copying Binary Files

```
File src = new File("src.jpg")
new File("dest.jpg").withOutputStream{ out ->
  out.write src.readBytes()
}
```

The majority of the convenience methods Groovy adds to java.io.File are geared toward text files. Luckily, binary files aren't completely ignored. Calling withOutputStream allows you to write binary data within the closure, knowing that all that silly flush() and close() nonsense is already taken care of.

Of course, this method works for text files as well. What you sacrifice in brevity you gain back in a generic algorithm that can be used for any file, regardless of type.

Copying Files Using the Underlying Operating System

```
File src = new File("src.jpg")
File dest = new File("dest.jpg")
"cp ${src.name} ${dest.name}".execute()
```

Using what we discussed in Section 5.4, *Running a Shell Command*, on page 80, letting your operating system do the heavy lifting makes quick work of copying files. You lose platform independence using this method, but you gain the full capabilities of the underlying operating system. Sometimes abstractions like java.io.File are helpful; other times they get in the way.

Adding Your Own Copy Method to File

```
File.metaClass.copy = {String destName ->
  if(delegate.isFile()){
    new File(destName).withOutputStream{ out ->
      out.write delegate.readBytes()
    }
  }
}
```

```
new File("src.jpg").copy("dest.jpg")
```

Now that we've explored several ways to copy files, you can add the method of your choice directly to the java.io.File object. (For more information, see Section 10.11, *Adding Methods to a Class Dynamically (ExpandoMetaClass)*, on page 190)

6.5 Using AntBuilder to Copy a File

```
def ant = new AntBuilder()
ant.copy(file:"src.txt", tofile:"dest.txt")
```

Anything that can be expressed in the traditional Ant XML format (usually found in a file named build.xml) can also be expressed in Groovy code using an groovy.util.AntBuilder. (See Chapter 8, *Writing XML*, on page 127 for more on easily working with XML using Groovy *builders*.) Since the underlying Ant JARs are included with Groovy, you don't even need to have Ant installed on your system to take advantage of AntBuilder.

In this example, we're taking the <copy> task from Ant and using it in Groovy. (A great place to see all the core Ant tasks and their parameters is in the online documentation.[3]) Here is what this task looks like in its native Ant dialect:

```
// build.xml
<project name="test" basedir=".">
  <target name="copy">
    <copy file="src.txt" tofile="dest.txt" />
  </target>
</project>
```

```
$ ant copy
Buildfile: build.xml
copy:
     [copy] Copying 1 file to /
BUILD SUCCESSFUL
Total time: 0 seconds
```

---

3. http://ant.apache.org/manual/index.html

Creating an AntBuilder object in Groovy implicitly takes care of the boilerplate <project> and <target> code, much like a Groovy script takes care of the boilerplate public class and public static void main(String[] args), as discussed in Section 5.3, *Accepting Command-Line Arguments*, on page 79. After that, ant.copy(file:"src.txt", tofile:"dest.txt") mirrors the Ant XML, albeit in MarkupBuilder dialect.

It initially might seem strange to use Ant for things other than building Java projects. But if you think about it for just a moment, <javac> is only one of the many tasks that Ant supports natively. If Ant provides convenient tasks for copying, moving, renaming, and deleting files—all implemented in Java, therefore ensuring cross-platform compliance, I might add—why not take advantage of it? If you already are familiar with the common Ant tasks, this is a way you can reuse your existing knowledge rather than learning Yet Another API.

Copying a File to a Directory

```
def ant = new AntBuilder()
ant.copy(file:"src.txt", todir:"../backup")
```

Another nicety that Ant offers is the ability to copy a file to a directory. If you want the filename to remain the same, this cuts down on a bit of repetition.

Overwriting the Destination File

```
def ant = new AntBuilder()
ant.copy(file:"src.txt", tofile:"dest.txt", overwrite:true)
```

By default, Ant will not overwrite the destination file if it is newer than the source file. To force the copy to happen, use the overwrite attribute.

6.6 Using AntBuilder to Copy a Directory

```
def ant = new AntBuilder()
ant.copy(todir:"backup"){
  fileset(dir:"images")
}

// build.xml
<project name="test" basedir=".">
  <target name="backupImages">
    <copy todir="backup">
      <fileset dir="images" />
    </copy>
  </target>
</project>
```

To copy an entire directory of files (including subdirectories), you need to use a nested fileset. Notice that the nested XML shows up as a nested closure in Groovy.

Selectively Including/Excluding Files

```
//NOTE: this WILL NOT copy files in subdirectories
// due to the pattern in include and exclude
def ant = new AntBuilder()
ant.copy(todir:"backup", overwrite:true){
  fileset(dir:"images"){
    include(name:"*.jpg")
    exclude(name:"*.txt")
  }
}
```

Expanding the fileset allows you to selectively include and exclude files based on pattern matching.

In accordance with Ant rules, the pattern *.jpg copies only those files in the parent directory. Files in subdirectories will not be copied unless you change the pattern to **/*.jpg:

```
//NOTE: this WILL copy files in subdirectories
// due to the pattern in include and exclude
def ant = new AntBuilder()
ant.copy(todir:"backup", overwrite:true){
  fileset(dir:"images"){
    include(name:"**/*.jpg")
    exclude(name:"**/*.txt")
  }
}
```

Flattening the Directory Structure on Copy

```
def ant = new AntBuilder()
ant.copy(todir:"backup", overwrite:true, flatten:true){
  fileset(dir:"images"){
    include(name:"**/*.jpg")
    exclude(name:"**/*.txt")
  }
}

// images (before):
images/logo.jpg
images/big_image.jpg
images/icons/button.jpg
images/icons/arrow.jpg
images/thumbnails/big_image_thumb.jpg
```

```
// backup (after):
backup/logo.jpg
backup/big_image.jpg
backup/button.jpg
backup/arrow.jpg
backup/big_image_thumb.jpg
```

Ant offers a quirky little attribute called flatten on the <copy> task. Let's assume you have files in images, images/icons, and images/thumbnails. If you want to consolidate them all to the backup directory without preserving the nested directory structure, you set the flatten attribute to true. Of course, bear in mind that you run the risk of filename collisions when you copy from many different directories into a single one. Remember to set the overwrite attribute appropriately.

6.7 Moving/Renaming Files

```
// using the File method
File src = new File("src.txt")
src.renameTo(new File("dest.txt"))

// using the operating system
"mv src.txt dest.txt".execute()

// using AntBuilder
def ant = new AntBuilder()
ant.move(file:"src.txt", tofile:"dest.txt")
```

After Section 6.4, *Copying Files*, on page 99 and Section 6.5, *Using AntBuilder to Copy a File*, on page 100, this section might be a bit anticlimactic. You can move files using the standard JDK File.renameTo method. You can also shell out to your operating system. You can also use the AntBuilder.move method. They all do the same thing—it's a matter of personal preference which technique you use.

6.8 Deleting Files

```
// using the File method
new File("src.txt").delete()

// using the operating system
"rm src.txt".execute()

// using AntBuilder
def ant = new AntBuilder()
ant.delete(file:"src.txt")
```

The techniques covered in Section 6.4, *Copying Files*, on page 99 and Section 6.5, *Using AntBuilder to Copy a File*, on page 100 apply equally well here. You can use the standard JDK File.delete method. You can also shell out to your operating system. You can also use the AntBuilder. delete method.

Deleting a Directory

```
def ant = new AntBuilder()
ant.delete(dir:"tmp")
```

Just like with AntBuilder.copy, you can delete either an individual file or a directory. Remember that AntBuilder.copy won't overwrite a newer destination file? Well, AntBuilder.delete won't delete empty directories unless you explicitly ask it to do so:

```
def ant = new AntBuilder()
ant.delete(dir:"tmp", includeemptydirs:"true")
```

Deleting Selected Files from a Directory

```
def ant = new AntBuilder()
ant.delete{
  fileset(dir:"tmp", includes:"**/*.bak")
}
```

The same nested filesets we used in Section 6.6, *Using AntBuilder to Copy a Directory*, on page 101 work here as well. Remember that *.bak will delete only the files in the current directory; **/*.bak recursively deletes files all the way down the directory tree.

6.9 Creating a ZIP File/Tarball

```
def ant = new AntBuilder()

// zip files
ant.zip(basedir:"images", destfile:"../backup.zip")

// tar files
ant.tar(basedir:"images", destfile:"../backup.tar")
ant.gzip(zipfile:"../backup.tar.gz", src:"../backup.tar")
ant.bzip2(zipfile:"../backup.tar.bz2", src:"../backup.tar")
```

AntBuilder comes to the rescue once again when it comes to creating ZIP files. The techniques described here are similar to what we saw in Section 6.5, *Using AntBuilder to Copy a File*, on page 100.

Notice that AntBuilder.zip compresses the files by default. To compress a .tar file, you should call AntBuilder.gzip or AntBuilder.bzip2. Gzip is the more common compression format of the two, but bzip2 tends to yield a smaller (more compressed) file.

Zipping Up Selected Files

```
def ant = new AntBuilder()
ant.zip(destfile:"../backup.zip"){
  fileset(dir:"images"){
    include(name:"**/*.jpg")
    exclude(name:"**/*.txt")
  }
}
```

The same nested filesets we discussed in Section 6.6, *Using AntBuilder to Copy a Directory*, on page 101 work here as well. Remember that *.jpg will zip up only those files in the current directory; **/*.jpg recursively zips up files all the way down the directory tree.

AntBuilder.tar supports the same nested fileset that you see here with AntBuilder.zip.

6.10 Unzipping/Untarring Files

```
def ant = new AntBuilder()

// unzip files
ant.unzip(src:"../backup.zip", dest:"/dest")

// untar files
ant.gunzip(src:"../backup.tar.gz")
ant.bunzip2(src:"../backup.tar.bz2")
ant.untar(src:"../backup.tar", dest:"/dest")
```

Not surprisingly, unzipping files looks much like what we discussed in Section 6.9, *Creating a ZIP File/Tarball*, on the facing page. If your tarball is compressed, you should gunzip or bunzip2 it as appropriate.

Unzipping Selected Files

```
def ant = new AntBuilder()
ant.unzip(src:"../backup.zip", dest:"/dest"){
  patternset{
    include(name:"**/*.jpg")
    exclude(name:"**/*.txt")
  }
}
```

This example is using a patternset in this example, although the same nested filesets that we discussed in Section 6.6, *Using AntBuilder to Copy a Directory*, on page 101 work here as well. Remember that *.jpg will unzip files only in the root of the zip file; **/*.jpg recursively unzips files all the way down the directory tree.

AntBuilder.untar supports the same nested patternset you can see here with AntBuilder.unzip.

Chapter 7

Parsing XML

Groovy makes working with XML a breeze. Of course, you can still use the tried-and-true Java XML libraries in your toolkit, but once you experience Groovy's native parsers and slurpers, you'll wonder why you used anything else. Groovy minimizes the divide between XML and code, making XML feel like a natural extension of the language.

For some real-world examples of how to use your newfound XML parsing skills, see Chapter 9, *Web Services*, on page 143.

7.1 The "I'm in a Hurry" Guide to Parsing XML

```
def p = """<person id="99">John Smith</person>"""
def person = new XmlSlurper().parseText(p)

println person
===> John Smith
println person.@id
===> 99
```

The quickest way to deal with XML in Groovy is to slurp it up using an XmlSlurper. As this example shows, you get the text of an element by simply asking for it by name. To get an attribute value, you ask for it using an @ and the attribute name.

Notice in this example how nicely Groovy heredocs work with XML? You don't have to worry about multiple lines or escaping internal quotes. Everything is stored right in the pString variable. Whenever I'm dealing with XML, HTML, JSON, or any other format that might have embedded quotes, I simply wrap 'em up in triple quotes. See Section 3.12, *Heredocs (Triple Quotes)*, on page 46 for more information.

```
def p2 = """
<person id="100">
  <firstname>Jane</firstname>
  <lastname>Doe</lastname>
  <address type="home">
    <street>123 Main St</street>
    <city>Denver</city>
    <state>CO</state>
    <zip>80020</zip>
  </address>
</person>"""

def person = new XmlSlurper().parseText(p2)
println person.firstname
===> Jane
println person.address.city
===> Denver
println person.address.@type
===> home
```

XmlSlurper allows you to navigate any arbitrarily deep XML structure by simply asking for the nodes by name. For example, person.address.city corresponds to <person><address><city>.

There are many subtle nuances to the Groovy/XML relationship. We'll introduce a second parser—the XmlParser—that complements the Xml-Slurper in the next section. They can be either confusingly similar or maddeningly different, depending on your point of view. We'll spend the rest of this chapter comparing and contrasting them. If, however, all you need to do is parse some simple XML and you don't want to think too much about it, you use an XmlSlurper and get on with your life.

7.2 Understanding the Difference Between XmlParser and XmlSlurper

```
def p = """"<person id="99">John Smith</person>"""

// XmlParser (*** different ***)
def person = new XmlParser().parseText(p)
println person.getClass()
===> class groovy.util.Node

// XmlSlurper (*** different ***)
person = new XmlSlurper().parseText(p)
println person.getClass()
===> class groovy.util.slurpersupport.NodeChild
```

Different or Same?

Understanding the differences between XmlParser and XmlSlurper can be a tricky business. Sometimes the differences are blatant—*this* call will work only on *that* class. Other times, the differences can be quite subtle. Of course, many times because of happy coincidence the two classes operate in the same way.

To help clarify things, I'll flag code as (*** different ***) or (*** same ***) when I show you XmlParser and XmlSlurper in the same example. Usually I'm trying to make one point or the other: "Hey, look at how much these two are alike!" or "Here is an important distinction between the two."

Groovy offers two native XML parsers: groovy.util.XmlParser and groovy.util. XmlSlurper. Their APIs are almost identical, which is a never-ending source of confusion. ("What is the difference?" "Which one should I use?" "Why on Earth would I have two classes that do the same thing?") The answer is, of course, that they don't do *exactly* the same thing. They are both XML parsing libraries, but each takes a slightly different approach to the problem.

An XmlParser thinks of the document in terms of nodes. When you start dealing with more complex XML documents in just a moment, XmlParser will return a List of nodes as you navigate the tree.

XmlSlurper, on the other hand, treats the document as a groovy.util. slurpersupport.GPathResult. (Since GPathResult is an abstract class, you can see groovy.util.slurpersupport.NodeChild show up as the implementation.) GPath is like XPath,[1] only with a "groovier" syntax. XPath uses slash notation to navigate deeply nested XML trees—GPath uses dots to do the same thing.

We're going to dig much deeper into these ideas throughout the chapter. For right now, though, think of XmlParser as a way to deal with the nodes of the XML document. Think of XmlSlurper as a way to deal with the data itself in terms of a query result.

```
<person id="99">John Smith</person>
```

---

1. http://en.wikipedia.org/wiki/Xpath

If you look at this XML snippet and see a person whose value is John Smith, then you are thinking like an XmlSlurper. If, instead, you see a root node whose text() method should return the String John Smith, then you are definitely more in the mind-set of an XmlParser. For a really good example of why the differing worldviews of the two parsers matter, see Section 7.8, *Navigating Deeply Nested XML*, on page 118.

You might be thinking, "Why not just marshal the XML directly into a GroovyBean? Then you can call getters and setters on the object." If that's the case, skip directly to Section 7.10, *Populating a GroovyBean from XML*, on page 125, or look at projects like JAXB[2] or Castor.[3] I agree that if you are using XML as a serialization or persistence format, getting to a bean representation of the data is something you should do as quickly as possible. But this chapter's primary focus is on getting the XML into Groovy in such a way that you can work with it programmatically. There are plenty of XML files out there such as server.xml, web.xml, and struts-config.xml where it is probably sufficient to deal with them as ad hoc XML Groovy objects and leave it at that.

Understanding XmlParser

```
def p = """<person id="100">Jane Doe</person>"""
def person = new XmlParser().parseText(p)

println person.text()
===> Jane Doe
println person.attribute("id")
===> 100
println person.attribute("foo")
===> null
```

XmlParser.parseText() returns a groovy.util.Node. A Node is a great class for holding things like XML elements. There is a text() method that returns the body of the node. There is an attribute() method that accepts a name and returns the given attribute. If you ask for an attribute that doesn't exist, attribute() returns null. Pretty straightforward, right?

The important thing to notice is that you are making method calls on an object. There is no illusion of dealing with the XML directly. You call the text() method to return text. You call the attribute() method to return the attribute.

---

2. http://en.wikipedia.org/wiki/JAXB
3. http://castor.org

If you prefer using Java libraries such as JDOM for programmatically working with XML, XmlParser will make you feel right at home.

You should also note that I named the node person to match the element name in the XML document. This is simply a convention that helps blur the distinction between the XML and the Groovy code. Technically, you could have just as easily named the node foo and called foo.text() to return Jane Doe. XML isn't a native datatype in Groovy (or in Java, for that matter), but cleverly naming your variables helps minimize the cognitive disconnect.

Understanding XmlSlurper

```
def p = """<person id="100">Jane Doe</person>"""
def person = new XmlSlurper().parseText(p)

println person
===> Jane Doe
println person.@id
===> 100
println person.@foo
===> (returns an empty string)
```

XmlSlurper.parseText() returns a groovy.util.slurpersupport.GPathResult. Technically this is a special class, but for now I'd like for you to think of it as simply the String result of a GPath query. In this example, asking for person returns the result of a query—the text (or body) of that element. If you are familiar with XPath, you know that @ is used to query for attributes. Asking for person.@id returns 100.

XmlSlurper is a null-safe XML parser. Asking for person.@foo (an attribute that doesn't exist) returns an empty string. Asking for person.bar (a node that doesn't exist) returns an empty string as well. This saves you from needlessly mucking up your code with try/catch blocks to protect you from the dreaded unchecked NullPointerException. XmlParser throws nulls at you in both cases.

The important thing to notice here is that it feels like we are dealing with the XML directly. There are no apparent method calls (although this is simply a metaprogramming head trick the Groovy developers are playing on you). You'll be much happier if you don't think too hard and spoil the illusion. The best way to keep XmlSlurper distinct from XmlParser is thinking of the latter as dealing with an API and the former as dealing with the XML directly. Trust me.

What, you don't trust me? You still want to know how XmlParser handles calls like person.firstname and person.lastname when firstname and lastname aren't compiled parts of the API? See Section 10.8, *Calling Methods That Don't Exist (invokeMethod)*, on page 185 for more information.

7.3 Parsing XML Documents

```
def file = new File("person.xml")
def url = "http://somewhere.org/person.xml"

// XmlParser (*** same ***)
def person = new XmlParser().parse(file)
def person2 = new XmlParser().parse(url)

// XmlSlurper (*** same ***)
person = new XmlSlurper().parse(file)
person2 = new XmlSlurper().parse(url)
```

Both XmlParser and XmlSlurper share identical parse() methods. You can pass parse() either a File or a String representing a URL—all the transportation mechanics are handled for you behind the scenes. See the API documentation at http://groovy.codehaus.org/api/ for more examples of the overloaded parse() method accepting an InputSource, an InputStream, and a Reader.

Parsing XML Strings

```
def p = """<person id="99">John Smith</person>"""

// XmlParser (*** same ***)
def person = new XmlParser().parseText(p)

// XmlSlurper (*** same ***)
person = new XmlSlurper().parseText(p)
```

Since the overloaded parse() method that accepts a String treats it as a URL, there is a separate parseText() method that you can use if you already have the XML stored in a String variable. We'll use parseText() in most examples in this section, only because the XML is inline with the rest of the code for clarity and copy/paste friendliness.

7.4 Dealing with XML Attributes

```
def p = """<person id="99" ssn="555-11-2222">John Smith</person>"""
```

```
// XmlParser (*** same ***)
def person = new XmlParser().parseText(p)
println person.attributes()
===> ["ssn":"555-11-2222", "id":"99"]

person.attributes().each{name, value->
  println "${name} ${value}"
}
===>
ssn 555-11-2222
id 99

// XmlSlurper (*** same ***)
person = new XmlSlurper().parseText(p)
println person.attributes()
===> ["ssn":"555-11-2222", "id":"99"]

person.attributes().each{name, value->
  println "${name} ${value}"
}
===>
ssn 555-11-2222
id 99
```

Attributes are the XML equivalent of Java hashmaps—they are a series of name/value pairs on the XML element. Both Node and GPathResult have an identical attributes() method that returns a hashmap. See Section 3.15, *Map Shortcuts*, on page 52 for all of the tricks you can do with a hashmap.

Getting a Single Attribute

```
def p = """<person id="99" ssn="555-11-2222">John Smith</person>"""

// XmlParser (*** different ***)
def person = new XmlParser().parseText(p)
println person.attribute("id")
===> 99
println person.attribute("foo")
===> null

// XmlSlurper (*** different ***)
person = new XmlSlurper().parseText(p)
println person.@id
===> 99
println person.@foo
===> (returns an empty string)
```

When using an XmlParser, you use the attribute() method to pull out individual attributes. When using an XmlSlurper, you use the @ notation directly on the attribute name.

Using Hashmap Syntax for Attributes

```
def p = """<person id="99" ssn="555-11-2222">John Smith</person>"""

// XmlParser (*** same ***)
def person = new XmlParser().parseText(p)
println person["@id"]
===> 99

def atts = ["id", "ssn"]
atts.each{att->
  println person["@${att}"]
}
===>
99
555-11-2222

// XmlSlurper (*** same ***)
person = new XmlSlurper().parseText(p)
println person["@id"]
===> 99

atts.each{att->
  println person["@${att}"]
}
===>
99
555-11-2222
```

Both XmlParser and XmlSlurper support an identical alternate syntax for attributes. Using hashmap notation (person["@id"]) is an ideal way to either blur the distinction between these two libraries or thoroughly confuse yourself if you're trying to tell them apart.

The best use I've found for this alternate hashmap syntax is for when I need to pull out an attribute based on a generic variable. Knowing that both classes support the same syntax—println person["@${att}"]—means I don't have to think too hard about the matter. I just use the syntax that works in both cases.

Of course, in the case of XmlParser, you can just as easily ask for person.attribute("${att}"). In the case of XmlSlurper, you can ask for person."@${att}".

7.5 Getting the Body of an XML Element

```
def p = """<person id="100">Jane Doe</person>"""

// XmlParser (*** different ***)
def person = new XmlParser().parseText(p)
println person.text()
===> Jane Doe

// XmlSlurper (*** different ***)
person = new XmlSlurper().parseText(p)
println person
===> Jane Doe
```

Getting text out of an XML element requires slightly different syntax from XmlParser and XmlSlurper. Recall from Section 7.2, *Understanding the Difference Between XmlParser and XmlSlurper*, on page 108 that each has a slightly different worldview. XmlSlurper treats everything like a big GPath query. Asking for an element such as person is tacitly asking for its text. XmlParser, on the other hand, treats everything like a node. You have to call text() on the node. If you don't, you are calling toString(), which returns debug output:

```
def p = """<person id="100">Jane Doe</person>"""
def person = new XmlParser().parseText(p)
println person
===> person[attributes={id=100}; value=[Jane Doe]]
```

Using Hashmap Syntax for Elements

```
def p = """
<person id="100">
  <firstname>Jane</firstname>
  <lastname>Doe</lastname>
</person>"""

// XmlParser (*** different ***)
def person = new XmlParser().parseText(p)
println person['firstname'].text()
===> Jane

// XmlSlurper (*** different ***)
person = new XmlSlurper().parseText(p)
println person['firstname']
===> Jane
```

Both parsers allow you to treat each child XML node as if it were a Map element of its parent. Calling person.firstname.text() or person['firstname'].text() (in the case of XmlParser) is purely a stylistic choice on your part, although sometimes the Map syntax is easier to work with if you have a List of element names to deal with:

```
def xml = """
<person id="100">
  <firstname>Jane</firstname>
  <lastname>Doe</lastname>
</person>
"""

def person = new XmlParser().parseText(xml)
def elements = ["firstname", "lastname"]
elements.each{element->
  println person[element].text()
}
===>
Jane
Doe
```

7.6 Dealing with Mixed-Case Element Names

```
// notice the case difference in firstname and LastName
// Groovy code mirrors the case of the XML element name
def p = """
<person id="99">
  <firstname>John</firstname>
  <LastName>Smith</LastName>
</person>
"""

// XmlParser (*** different ***)
def person = new XmlParser().parseText(p)
println person.firstname.text()
===> John
println person.LastName.text()
===> Smith

// XmlSlurper (*** different ***)
person = new XmlSlurper().parseText(p)
println person.firstname
===> John
println person.LastName
===> Smith
```

Neither XML parser cares whether the XML element names are lower-case, uppercase, or mixed case. You reference them in Groovy the same way they show up in the XML file.

7.7 Dealing with Hyphenated Element Names

```
//notice the hyphenated and underscored element names
//Groovy has to use special syntax to deal with the hyphens
def p = """
<person id="99">
  <first-name>John</first-name>
  <last_name>Smith</last_name>
</person>
"""

// XmlParser (*** different ***)
def person = new XmlParser().parseText(p)
println person.first-name.text()
===>
Caught: groovy.lang.MissingPropertyException:
No such property: name for class: person

println person.'first-name'.text()
println person['first-name'].text()
===>
John

println person.last_name.text()
println person.'last_name'.text()
println person['last_name'].text()
===>
Smith

// XmlSlurper (*** different ***)
person = new XmlSlurper().parseText(p)
println person.'first-name'
println person['first-name']
===>
John

println person.last_name
println person.'last_name'
println person['last_name']
===>
Smith
```

Both XML parsers do their best to blur the distinction between XML and
Groovy, mirroring the node names wherever possible. Unfortunately, in
certain edge cases this facade breaks down when naming rules don't
match up 100%. (This is known as a *leaky abstraction*.[4])

---

4. http://en.wikipedia.org/wiki/Leaky_abstraction

Although hyphenated names are perfectly valid in XML, person.first-name in Groovy means "take the value of the variable name and subtract it from person.first." Surrounding the hyphenated name with quotes turns the statement back into a valid Groovy construct.

Notice, however, that names with underscores can be used as is. Underscores are valid in both Groovy and XML, so you can leave the quotes off in Groovy. Move along, people—there's nothing to see. No leaky abstractions here.

7.8 Navigating Deeply Nested XML

```
def p = """
<person id="100">
  <firstname>Jane</firstname>
  <lastname>Doe</lastname>
  <address type="home">
    <street>123 Main St</street>
    <city>Denver</city>
    <state>CO</state>
    <zip>80020</zip>
  </address>
</person>"""

// XmlParser (*** different ***)
def person = new XmlParser().parseText(p)
println person.address[0].street[0].text()
===> 123 Main St

// XmlSlurper (*** different ***)
person = new XmlSlurper().parseText(p)
println person.address.street
===> 123 Main St
```

Since the beginning of the chapter, I've been trying to tell you how different these two libraries are. Now, for the first time, you can really see the two different worldviews manifest themselves.

XmlParser sees the XML document as an ArrayList of nodes. This means you have to use array notation all the way down the tree. XmlSlurper sees the XML document as one big GPath query waiting to happen. Let's explore each in greater detail.

XmlParser: text(), children(), and value()

```
def p = """
<person id="100">
  <firstname>Jane</firstname>
  <lastname>Doe</lastname>
  <address type="home">
    <street>123 Main St</street>
    <city>Denver</city>
    <state>CO</state>
    <zip>80020</zip>
  </address>
</person>"""

def person = new XmlParser().parseText(p)
println person.text()
===> (returns an empty string)

println person.children()
===>
[
  firstname[attributes={}; value=[Jane]],
  lastname[attributes={}; value=[Doe]],
  address[attributes={type=home}; value=[
    street[attributes={}; value=[123 Main St]],
    city[attributes={}; value=[Denver]],
    state[attributes={}; value=[CO]],
    zip[attributes={}; value=[80020]]
  ]]
]

println person.value()
// A generic function that returns either text() or value(),
// depending on which field is populated.
// In this case, person.value() is equivalent to children().
```

We have talked about the text() method already. Now it's time to introduce the other Node method you'll use quite frequently: children(). Although text() returns a String, children() returns an ArrayList of nodes. If you think about it, a node in an XML document can have only one or the other. Person has children; firstname has text. Address has children; city has text.

Understanding the dual nature of Node—coupled with a bit of Groovy truth (as discussed in Section 3.10, *Groovy Truth*, on page 44)—makes it trivial to determine whether a node is a leaf or a branch. This allows you to recurse through a document of any arbitrary depth quite simply.

```
if(person.text()){
        println "Leaf"
} else{
        println "Branch"
}
===> Branch

if(person.children()){
        println "Branch"
} else{
        println "Leaf"
}
===> Branch
```

The final method on Node you should be familiar with is value(). This method returns either text() or children(), depending on which is populated.

XmlParser: each()

```
def p = """
<person id="100">
  <firstname>Jane</firstname>
  <lastname>Doe</lastname>
  <address type="home">
    <street>123 Main St</street>
    <city>Denver</city>
    <state>CO</state>
    <zip>80020</zip>
  </address>
  <address type="work">
    <street>987 Other Ave</street>
    <city>Boulder</city>
    <state>CO</state>
    <zip>80090</zip>
  </address>
</person>"""

def person = new XmlParser().parseText(p)

println person.address[0].attribute("type")
===> home
println person.address[1].attribute("type")
===> work
person.address.each{a->
  println a.attribute("type")
}
===>
home
work
```

Since children() returns an ArrayList of nodes, you can use all the tricks you learned in Section 3.14, *List Shortcuts*, on page 48 to deal with them. You can use array notation to get at the specific address you are interested in, or you can use each() to iterate through the list.

When navigating the tree using XmlParser, the syntax reminds you at every turn that each child node could potentially be one of many. In the following example, we walk through each address in the document and ask for the first city found. In this particular case, it's kind of a bummer—logically it doesn't make sense for an address to have more than one city, but there is no XML rule that would preclude it from happening. Therefore, you must trap for it explicitly:

```
person.address.each{a->
  println a.city[0].text()
}
===>
Denver
Boulder
```

On the positive side, XmlParser makes it trivial to take a vertical slice through your XML. If you simply want every city across all addresses, this code makes short work of it:

```
person.address.city.each{c->
  println c.text()
}
===>
Denver
Boulder
```

I hope this section makes it abundantly clear that XmlParser considers your XML document to be nothing more than nodes and lists of nodes.

XmlSlurper

```
def p = """
<person id="100">
  <firstname>Jane</firstname>
  <lastname>Doe</lastname>
  <address type="home">
    <street>123 Main St</street>
    <city>Denver</city>
    <state>CO</state>
    <zip>80020</zip>
  </address>
</person>"""

def person = new XmlSlurper().parseText(p)
println person.firstname
===> Jane
```

```
println person.lastname
===> Doe
println person.address.city
===> Denver
```

Whereas XmlParser treats everything like a node or a list of nodes, Xml-Slurper treats everything like the result of a GPath query. This makes it more natural to navigate the path. When you ask for person.address.city, you are implicitly asking for the text in that element. Stated another way, XmlParser has a strong affinity for branches. XmlSlurper is exactly the opposite: it is optimized for leaves.

Of course, sometimes your query results can end up being looking like nonsense if you aren't specific enough:

```
println person
===> JaneDoe123 Main StDenverCO80020
println person.address
===> 123 Main StDenverCO80020
```

In each case, you were asking for a branch instead of a leaf. Making sure you always are asking for a specific leaf will help ensure you get the results you want. In the following example, you have to ask for the city of a specific address in order to get a reasonable response:

```
def p = """
<person id="100">
  <firstname>Jane</firstname>
  <lastname>Doe</lastname>
  <address type="home">
    <street>123 Main St</street>
    <city>Denver</city>
    <state>CO</state>
    <zip>80020</zip>
  </address>
  <address type="work">
    <street>987 Other Ave</street>
    <city>Boulder</city>
    <state>CO</state>
    <zip>80090</zip>
  </address>
</person>"""

def person = new XmlSlurper().parseText(p)
println person.address.city
===>DenverBoulder
println person.address[0].city
===>Denver
```

On the other hand, if you truly want a vertical slice of all cities, you can walk through each of them as you would any other list:

```
person.address.city.each{println it}
===>
Denver
Boulder
```

7.9 Parsing an XML Document with Namespaces

```
def p_xml = """
<p:person
    xmlns:p="http://somewhere.org/person"
    xmlns:xsi="http://www.w3.org/2001/XMLSchema-instance"
    xsi:schemaLocation="http://somewhere.org/person
                        http://somewhere.org/person.xsd"
    id="99">
  <p:firstname>John</p:firstname>
  <p:last-name>Smith</p:last-name>
</p:person>
"""

def person = new XmlParser().parseText(p_xml)

//the firstname element cannot be found without its namespace
println person.firstname.text()
===> []

def p = new groovy.xml.Namespace("http://somewhere.org/person")
println person[p.firstname].text()
===> John

println person[p.'last-name'].text()
===> Smith
```

When people grumble about XML, namespaces usually top the list. "It complicates things," they mutter under their breath. The benefits of namespaces are, of course, that you can produce an XML document that represents a complex domain. Consider a document that has name elements used in different contexts:

```
<product:name>iPhone</product:name>
<vendor:name>Apple</vendor:name>
```

An alternative to namespacing the name elements is to make them unique in the default namespace, but this might not be possible if you are merging XML from disparate sources.

```
<product-name>iPhone</product-name>
<vendor-name>Apple</vendor-name>
```

Thankfully, Groovy makes dealing with namespaces as unobtrusive as possible. You simply declare the namespace and then prefix all your element references with the namespace variable:

```
def p = new groovy.xml.Namespace("http://somewhere.org/person")
println person[p.firstname].text()
===> John
```

Since the dot operator is used to traverse the tree, asking for person. p.firstname would be ambiguous. When dealing with namespaced elements, you can use only the HashMap notation, as discussed in Section 7.5, *Using Hashmap Syntax for Elements*, on page 115: person[p.firstname].text(). You simply quote the element name: person[p. 'last-name'].text(), if you have hyphenated elements that are also namespaced.

Namespaces in XmlSlurper

```
def p = """
<p:person
    xmlns:p="http://somewhere.org/person"
    xmlns:xsi="http://www.w3.org/2001/XMLSchema-instance"
    xsi:schemaLocation="http://somewhere.org/person
                        http://somewhere.org/person.xsd"
    id="99">
  <p:firstname>John</p:firstname>
  <p:last-name>Smith</p:last-name>
</p:person>
"""

def person = new XmlSlurper().parseText(p)
println person.firstname
println person.'last-name'
===>
John
Smith
```

XmlSlurper differs from XmlParser when it comes to XML namespaces. XmlSlurper, by default, ignores all namespaces, whereas XmlParser pays attention to them. This makes it easy to rip through an XML document in a loose (if not completely valid) way.XmlSlurper will respect namespaces if you tell it about them. The GPathResult class has a declare-Namespace() method that takes a Map of namespaces.

```
def itemXml = """
<item
  xmlns:product="urn:somecompany:products"
  xmlns:vendor="urn:somecompany:vendors">
    <product:name>iPhone</product:name>
```

```
      <vendor:name>Apple</vendor:name>
      <quantity>1</quantity>
</item>
"""

def item = new XmlSlurper().parseText(itemXml)
println item.name
===> iPhoneApple

def ns = [:]
ns.product = "urn:somecompany:products"
ns.vendor = "urn:somecompany:vendors"
item.declareNamespace(ns)

println item.'product:name'
===> iPhone
```

Without the namespaces declared, calling the name element returns *both* names. Once the GPathResult knows about the namespaces, it will allow you to call properly qualified elements.

Did you notice that XmlParser makes you use a dot between the namespace and the element name? XmlSlurper, once again, comes closer to matching the original XML syntax. item.'product:name' corresponds to <item><product:name> using the same symbol: the colon. Unfortunately, a colon isn't a legal character in a variable name. In XmlSlurper, you need to surround namespaced element names in quotes.

7.10 Populating a GroovyBean from XML

```
def p = """
<person>
  <firstname>Jane</firstname>
  <lastname>Doe</lastname>
</person>
"""

class Person{
  String firstname
  String lastname
}

def pxml = new XmlParser().parseText(p)
def person = new Person()

pxml.children().each{child ->
  person.setProperty(child.name(), child.text())
}
```

Although this solution doesn't offer the richness of a true XML-to-Java marshaling solution such as Castor,[5] for the simplest possible case it's nice to know that you can easily construct a valid GroovyBean from XML.pxml.children() returns a list of nodes. Each Node has a name() method and a text() method. Using the native setProperty method on the GroovyBean makes short work of constructing a valid class from XML.

If you know you have a more deeply nested XML structure, you should call children() recursively. If you have attributes, you can call attributes() on each node to return a Map. (See Section 7.8, *XmlParser: text(), children(), and value()*, on page 119 for more tips on dynamic introspection of the structure of an XML document.) The point here is not to present a complete solution for every possible circumstance—the point is to show the possibilities of dealing with XML using everyday Groovy classes.

---

5. http://castor.org

Chapter 8

Writing XML

In Chapter 7, *Parsing XML*, on page 107, we explored different ways to ingest XML. (Doesn't "slurp" sound much cooler than "ingest" now that you know all about XmlSlurper?) In this chapter, we'll look at different ways to write XML.

As with Groovy parsers, you have two similar (yet subtly different) classes available to build XML documents—MarkupBuilder and StreamingMarkupBuilder. By the end of this chapter, you should have a much clearer idea of the strengths and weaknesses of each.

8.1 The "I'm in a Hurry" Guide to Creating an XML Document

```
def xml = new groovy.xml.MarkupBuilder()
xml.person(id:99){
  firstname("John")
  lastname("Smith")
}
===>
<person id='99'>
  <firstname>John</firstname>
  <lastname>Smith</lastname>
</person>
```

Like magic, XML documents seem to simply fall out of Groovy with ease. This is because of the dynamic nature of groovy.xml.MarkupBuilder. Methods such as person, firstname, and lastname look like they are native to MarkupBuilder, although half a second of thought will convince us that there is simply no way that MarkupBuilder could implement an entire dictionary of words as methods just to facilitate this. Instead, we have to give credit to our dynamic-enabling friend invokeMethod(), as discussed in Section 10.8, *Calling Methods That Don't Exist (invokeMethod)*, on page 185.

As you make methods calls on MarkupBuilder that do not exist, invokeMethod() catches those calls and interprets them as nodes for the XML document. name:value pairs passed in as arguments for the nonexistent methods are interpreted as attributes. (Groovy supports named arguments and variable-length argument lists, as discussed in Section 4.5, *Constructor Shortcut Syntax*, on page 66.) Values passed in without a name prefix are interpreted as the element's body. Nested closures correspond to nesting in the XML document.

Capturing Output

```
def sw = new StringWriter()
def xml = new groovy.xml.MarkupBuilder(sw)

def fw = new FileWriter("/path/to/some/file.xml")
def xml2 = new groovy.xml.MarkupBuilder(fw)
```

By default, MarkupBuilder echos the output to System.out. If you want to capture the output, an alternate constructor accepts a Writer. You can pass in a StringWriter to capture the output in memory, or you can use a FileWriter to write the results directly to file.

8.2 Creating Mixed-Case Element Names

```
def xml = new groovy.xml.MarkupBuilder()
xml.PERSON(id:100){
  firstName("Jane")
  LastName("Doe")
}

===>
<PERSON id='100'>
  <firstName>Jane</firstName>
  <LastName>Doe</LastName>
</PERSON>
```

As discussed in Section 7.6, *Dealing with Mixed-Case Element Names*, on page 116, your Groovy code is meant to match your XML output as closely as possible. Even though the odd cases in this example don't follow Java/Groovy coding conventions (classes begin with a capital letter, variables begin with a lowercase letter, and constants are in all caps), Groovy preserves the case so that your output is exactly as you'd expect it to be.

8.3 Creating Hyphenated Element Names

```
def xml = new groovy.xml.MarkupBuilder()
xml.person(id:99){
  "first-name"("John")
  last_name("Smith")
}


===>
<person id='99'>
  <first-name>John</first-name>
  <last_name>Smith</last_name>
</person>
```

As discussed in Section 7.7, *Dealing with Hyphenated Element Names*, on page 117, element names with hyphens are perfectly valid in XML but aren't valid in Groovy.

To create hyphenated XML element names using a MarkupBuilder, you simply surround the element name in quotes. Since underscores are valid in Groovy, the MarkupBuilder passes them through unchanged.

If you forget to surround a hyphenated name in quotes, you'll get an exception:

```
def xml = new groovy.xml.MarkupBuilder()
xml.person(id:99){
  first-name("John")
  last_name("Smith")
}


===>
Caught: groovy.lang.MissingPropertyException:
No such property: first for class: builder
```

8.4 Creating Namespaced XML Using MarkupBuilder

```
def xml = new groovy.xml.MarkupBuilder()
def params = [:]
params."xmlns:product" = "urn:somecompany:products"
params."xmlns:vendor" = "urn:somecompany:vendors"
params.id = 99
xml.person(params){
  "product:name"("iPhone")
  "vendor:name"("Apple")
  quantity(1)
}
```

```
===>
<person
  xmlns:product='urn:somecompany:products'
  xmlns:vendor='urn:somecompany:vendors'
  id='99'>
    <product:name>iPhone</product:name>
    <vendor:name>Apple</vendor:name>
    <quantity>1</quantity>
</person>
```

You can easily create XML documents with namespaces using a Markup-
Builder. Your namespace declarations in the root element are no different
from any other attributes. Your namespaced element names are no different from hyphenated element names—you simply surround them in
quotes.

OK, so technically MarkupBuilder doesn't understand namespaces, but
that doesn't stop it from blithely spitting out whatever you ask it to spit
out. In Section 8.7, *Creating Namespaced XML Using StreamingMarkup-
Builder*, on page 133, you can see a namespace-aware builder.

8.5 Understanding the Difference Between MarkupBuilder and StreamingMarkupBuilder

```
// MarkupBuilder
def xml = new groovy.xml.MarkupBuilder()
xml.person(id:100){
  firstname("Jane")
  lastname("Doe")
}
===>
<person id='100'>
  <firstname>Jane</firstname>
  <lastname>Doe</lastname>
</person>

// StreamingMarkupBuilder
def xml = new groovy.xml.StreamingMarkupBuilder().bind{
  person(id:100){
    firstname("Jane")
    lastname("Doe")
  }
}

println xml
===>
<person id='100'><firstname>Jane</firstname><lastname>Doe</lastname></person>
```

Like the siblings XmlParser and XmlSlurper we discussed in Section 7.2, *Understanding the Difference Between XmlParser and XmlSlurper*, on page 108, Groovy offers two ways to emit XML.

MarkupBuilder is the simpler, if more limited, of the two. StreamingMarkup-Builder is a class that you can reach for when your needs exceed what MarkupBuilder can offer.

There are three key differences between MarkupBuilder and Streaming-MarkupBuilder:

- MarkupBuilder sends its output to System.out by default; Streaming-MarkupBuilder is silent until you explicitly hand it off to a Writer.

- MarkupBuilder is synchronous; StreamingMarkupBuilder is asynchronous. In other words, MarkupBuilder writes the XML document out immediately. StreamingMarkupBuilder allows you to define the closure separately. The document is not generated until the StreamingMarkupBuilder is passed to a Writer.

- Finally, MarkupBuilder pretty-prints its output, whereas Streaming-MarkupBuilder does not. (All subsequent XML output from StreamingMarkupBuilder in this chapter will be pretty-printed for readability.) If you need to pretty-print the results, look to the command-line tool Tidy[1] (standard on most Unix/Linux/Mac systems, downloadable for Windows) or the Java library JTidy.[2]

The remainder of this chapter focuses on StreamingMarkupBuilder and the advanced capabilities it brings to the party.

8.6 Creating Parts of the XML Document Separately

```
def builder = new groovy.xml.StreamingMarkupBuilder()
def person = {
  person(id:99){
    firstname("John")
    lastname("Smith")
  }
}
println builder.bind(person)
===>
<person id='99'><firstname>John</firstname><lastname>Smith</lastname></person>
```

---

1. http://tidy.sourceforge.net/
2. http://jtidy.sourceforge.net/

StreamingMarkupBuilder allows you to define a closure and pass it in to
the bind() method. This means you can decouple the two—creating the
closure independently and binding it to the StreamingMarkupBuilder at
the exact moment you'd like to create the XML document.

If you can create a single closure independently, it only stands to reason that you can create many closures independently and pull them
together as needed:

```
def builder = new groovy.xml.StreamingMarkupBuilder()

def person1 = {
  person(id:99){
    firstname("John")
    lastname("Smith")
  }
}

def person2 = {
  person(id:100){
    firstname("Jane")
    lastname("Doe")
  }
}

def personList = {
  "person-list"{
    out << person1
    out << person2
  }
}

println builder.bind(personList)
===>
<person-list>
  <person id='99'>
    <firstname>John</firstname><lastname>Smith</lastname>
  </person>
  <person id='100'>
    <firstname>Jane</firstname><lastname>Doe</lastname>
  </person>
</person-list>
```

In this example, the personList closure contains references to two other
closures: person1 and person2. StreamingMarkupBuilder supplies an out
target to which you should point the embedded closures. Without
out, StreamingMarkupBuilder could not tell the difference between an element you want emitted (firstname) and a closure that needs to be
dereferenced.

8.7 Creating Namespaced XML Using StreamingMarkupBuilder

```
def builder = new groovy.xml.StreamingMarkupBuilder().bind{
  mkp.declareNamespace('':'http://myDefaultNamespace')
  mkp.declareNamespace('location':'http://someOtherNamespace')
  person(id:100){
    firstname("Jane")
    lastname("Doe")
    location.address("123 Main St")
  }
}
println builder
===>
<person id='100'
      xmlns='http://myDefaultNamespace'
      xmlns:location='http://someOtherNamespace'>
  <firstname>Jane</firstname>
  <lastname>Doe</lastname>
  <location:address>123 Main St</location:address>
</person>
```

In Section 8.4, *Creating Namespaced XML Using MarkupBuilder*, on page 129, we tricked MarkupBuilder into emitting namespaced XML elements even though technically it isn't namespace-aware. Streaming-MarkupBuilder, on the other hand, is namespace-aware. You pass in namespace declarations to the reserved namespace mkp. Anything prefixed with mkp is interpreted as internal instructions to the builder rather than output that should be emitted. Notice that location.address is emitted as location:address, while mkp.declareNamespace is nowhere to be found in the output. You specify the default namespace for the XML document by passing in an empty string as the key.

8.8 Printing Out the XML Declaration

```
def builder = new groovy.xml.StreamingMarkupBuilder()
def person = {
  mkp.xmlDeclaration()
}
println builder.bind(person)
===>
<?xml version="1.0" encoding="MacRoman"?>

//setting the encoding
def builder2 = new groovy.xml.StreamingMarkupBuilder()
builder2.encoding = "UTF-8"
println builder2.bind{
  mkp.xmlDeclaration()
}
===>
<?xml version="1.0" encoding="UTF-8"?>
```

The XML declaration is printed when you call xmlDeclaration() on the reserved mkp namespace. You can set the encoding directly on the instance of StreamingMarkupBuilder in order to override the default system encoding.

8.9 Printing Out Processing Instructions

```
def builder = new groovy.xml.StreamingMarkupBuilder()
def person = {
  mkp.pi("xml-stylesheet": "type='text/xsl' href='myfile.xslt'")
}
println builder.bind(person)
===>
<?xml-stylesheet type='text/xsl' href='myfile.xslt'?>
```

Processing instructions, like those used for XSLT, are printed when you call pi() on the reserved mkp namespace.

8.10 Printing Arbitrary Strings (Comments, CDATA)

```
def comment = "<!-- address is optional -->"
def builder = new groovy.xml.StreamingMarkupBuilder().bind{
  person(id:99){
    firstname("John")
    lastname("Smith")
    mkp.yieldUnescaped(comment)
    unescaped << comment
  }
}
println builder
===>
<person id='99'>
  <firstname>John</firstname>
  <lastname>Smith</lastname>
  <!-- address is optional -->
  <!-- address is optional -->
</person>
```

The reserved namespace mkp has played prominently in the past few sections. Calling mkp.declareNamespace() allows you to create namespaces of your own. Calling mkp.xmlDeclaration() dumps out an XML declaration. Calling mkp.pi() prints out processing instructions. Now you see another method call—mkp.yieldUnescaped(). As the name implies, this method prints the string you pass in unchanged. unescaped << is a convenience target that does the same thing. It is purely a stylistic decision as to which form you use.

If you want StreamingMarkupBuilder to escape the string for you, you call mkp.yield() or out <<. (Remember out from Section 8.6, *Creating Parts of the XML Document Separately*, on page 131?)

```
def comment = "<!-- address is optional -->"
def builder = new groovy.xml.StreamingMarkupBuilder().bind{
  mkp.yieldUnescaped(comment)
  unescaped << comment
  mkp.yield(comment)
  out << comment
}
println builder
===>
<!-- address is optional -->
<!-- address is optional -->
&lt;!-- address is optional --&gt;
&lt;!-- address is optional --&gt;
```

An interesting feature of mkp.yield() and out << is that it escapes Strings by default but passes other closures through unchanged. I've been bitten by this more than once if I flip between a String and a closure during the development process. The good news is both mkp.yieldUnescaped() and unescaped << pass a closure through unchanged as well. In other words, you can use out and unescaped interchangeably for closures. However, if you want to polymorphically flip between Strings and closures, unescaped is probably a better bet than out.

CDATA

```
def cdata = " >< & Look 'at' me & >< "
def builder = new groovy.xml.StreamingMarkupBuilder().bind{
  unescaped << "<![CDATA[" + cdata + "]]>"
}
println builder
===>
<![CDATA[ >< & Look 'at' me & >< ]]>
```

In XML, CDATA[3] sections are a hint to the parser to not treat the text as markup. Rather, it should be interpreted as plain old *character data*. Effectively, this means you can pass in characters that would ordinarily need to be escaped, such as <, >, &, and quotes (both single and double).

Although it would be especially convenient if a mkp.cdata() method call existed, you can achieve the same thing by using the humble unescaped target that you already know.

---

3. http://en.wikipedia.org/wiki/CDATA

8.11 Writing StreamingMarkupBuilder Output to a File

```
def writer = new FileWriter("person.xml")
writer << builder.bind(person)
```

You can pass the output of a StreamingMarkupBuilder to any Java class that implements the Writer interface.

8.12 StreamingMarkupBuilder at a Glance

```
def comment = "<!-- address is new to this release -->"
def builder = new groovy.xml.StreamingMarkupBuilder()
builder.encoding = "UTF-8"
def person = {
  mkp.xmlDeclaration()
  mkp.pi("xml-stylesheet": "type='text/xsl' href='myfile.xslt'" )
  mkp.declareNamespace('':'http://myDefaultNamespace')
  mkp.declareNamespace('location':'http://someOtherNamespace')
  person(id:100){
    firstname("Jane")
    lastname("Doe")
    mkp.yieldUnescaped(comment)
    location.address("123 Main")
  }
}
def writer = new FileWriter("person.xml")
writer << builder.bind(person)

System.out << builder.bind(person)
===>
<?xml version="1.0" encoding="UTF-8"?>
<?xml-stylesheet type='text/xsl' href='myfile.xslt'?>
<person id='100'
    xmlns='http://myDefaultNamespace'
    xmlns:location='http://someOtherNamespace'>
  <firstname>Jane</firstname>
  <lastname>Doe</lastname>
  <!-- address is new to this release -->
  <location:address>123 Main</location:address>
</person>
```

Putting everything together you've learned in the past several sections gives you the tools you need to build an XML document of any complexity. MarkupBuilder is still there for simple jobs, but StreamingMarkupBuilder is there when you need to do the complicated stuff.

8.13   Creating HTML on the Fly

```
def x = new groovy.xml.MarkupBuilder()
x.html{
  head{
    title("Search Results")
    link(rel:"stylesheet", type:"text/css", href:"http://main.css")
    script(type:"text/javascript", src:"http://main.js")
  }
  body{
    h1("Search Results")
    div(id:"results", class:"simple"){
      table(border:1){
        tr{
          th("Name")
          th("Address")
        }
        tr{
          td{
            a(href:"http://abc.org?id=100","Jane Doe")
          }
          td("123 Main St")
        }
      }
    }
  }
}
===>
<html>
  <head>
    <title>Search Results</title>
    <link rel='stylesheet' type='text/css' href='http://main.css' />
    <script type='text/javascript' src='http://main.js' />
  </head>
  <body>
    <h1>Search Results</h1>
    <div id='results' class='simple'>
      <table border='1'>
        <tr>
          <th>Name</th>
          <th>Address</th>
        </tr>
        <tr>
          <td>
            <a href='http://abc.org?id=100'>Jane Doe</a>
          </td>
          <td>123 Main St</td>
        </tr>
      </table>
    </div>
  </body>
</html>
```

MarkupBuilder is equally adept at emitting XML or HTML. In the previous example, I put together a quick HTML page.

Bear in mind that you're not in a full web framework like Grails. Grails operates at a much higher level of abstraction, making it far easier to emit HTML tables and the like. Groovy Server Pages (GSPs) are a much better templating solution than writing out all of your HTML in longhand as I did here, just as JSPs are generally better than having a series of System.out.println statements in the doGet() method of a Servlet. The point of this example is to demonstrate the DSL capabilities of Groovy. (See the sidebar on page 33 for more on DSLs.) The Groovy code matches the resulting HTML almost perfectly. For writing ad hoc HTML pages on the fly in Groovy, I haven't found anything better than good old MarkupBuilder.

HTML and StreamingMarkupBuilder

```
def h = {
  head{
    title("Search Results")
    link(rel:"stylesheet", type:"text/css", href:"http://main.css")
    script(type:"text/javascript", src:"http://main.js")
  }
}

def b = {
  body{
    h1("Search Results")
    div(id:"results", class:"simple"){
      table(border:1){
        tr{
          th("Name")
          th("Address")
        }
        tr{
          td{
            a(href:"http://abc.org?id=100","Jane Doe")
          }
          td("123 Main St")
        }
      }
    }
  }
}

def html = new groovy.xml.StreamingMarkupBuilder().bind{
  unescaped << '<!DOCTYPE HTML PUBLIC "-//W3C//DTD HTML 4.01//EN"' +
               '"http://www.w3.org/TR/html4/strict.dtd">'
  html{
    out << h
```

```
    out << b
  }
}

def htmlWriter = new FileWriter("test.html")
htmlWriter << html
```

Using StreamingMarkupBuilder, you are able to define blocks of the page asynchronously and pull them together just as you need them. This allows you to put together a more robust templating system.

8.14 Converting CSV to XML

```
// input file (addresses.csv):
99,John Smith,456 Fleet St,Denver,CO,80021
100,Jane Doe,123 Main St,Denver,CO,80020
101,Frank Jones,345 Center Blvd,Omaha,NE,68124

// groovy file:
def fileIn = new File("addresses.csv")
def fileOut = new FileWriter("addresses.xml")
def xml = new groovy.xml.MarkupBuilder(fileOut)
xml.addressBook{
  fileIn.splitEachLine(","){ tokens ->
    entry(id:tokens[0]){
      name(tokens[1])
      addresss(tokens[2])
      city(tokens[3])
      state(tokens[4])
      zipcode(tokens[5])
    }
  }
}

// output file (addresses.xml):
<addressBook>
  <entry id='99'>
    <name>John Smith</name>
    <addresss>456 Fleet St</addresss>
    <city>Denver</city>
    <state>CO</state>
    <zipcode>80021</zipcode>
  </entry>
  <entry id='100'>
    <name>Jane Doe</name>
    <addresss>123 Main St</addresss>
    <city>Denver</city>
    <state>CO</state>
    <zipcode>80020</zipcode>
  </entry>
```

```
    <entry id='101'>
      <name>Frank Jones</name>
      <addresss>345 Center Blvd</addresss>
      <city>Omaha</city>
      <state>NE</state>
      <zipcode>68124</zipcode>
    </entry>
</addressBook>
```

CSV files are quite common. Predating XML, CSV is yet another way to store data in a vendor-, language-, and platform-neutral way. Combining the splitEachLine() method discussed in Section 6.2, *Reading the Contents of a File*, on page 95 and the MarkupBuilder discussed in Section 8.1, *The "I'm in a Hurry" Guide to Creating an XML Document*, on page 127, you can easily convert CSV to XML.

Parsing Complex CSV

```
// input file
99,John Smith,"456 Fleet St, Suite 123",Denver,CO,80021
100,Jane Doe,123 Main St,Denver,CO,80020
101,"Frank Jones, Jr.",345 Center Blvd,Omaha,NE,68124

// output file
<addressBook>
  <entry id='99'>
    <name>John Smith</name>
    <addresss>"456 Fleet St</addresss>
    <city> Suite 123"</city>
    <state>Denver</state>
    <zipcode>CO</zipcode>
  </entry>
  <entry id='100'>
    <name>Jane Doe</name>
    <addresss>123 Main St</addresss>
    <city>Denver</city>
    <state>CO</state>
    <zipcode>80020</zipcode>
  </entry>
  <entry id='101'>
    <name>"Frank Jones</name>
    <addresss> Jr."</addresss>
    <city>345 Center Blvd</city>
    <state>Omaha</state>
    <zipcode>NE</zipcode>
  </entry>
</addressBook>
```

Unfortunately, CSV rarely presents itself as cleanly as it did in the first example. Sometimes there will be embedded commas in the field, requiring the entire field to be surrounded by quotes. (Did you catch the bad XML addresses for John Smith and Frank Jones, Jr.?)

You're going to need to do more than naively split the line on a comma to parse out these CSV records. Here is a slightly more robust CSV parsing class called SmartCsvParser that does a better job of dealing with embedded commas within individual CSV fields:

```groovy
def fileIn = new File("addresses2.csv")
def fileOut = new FileWriter("addresses2.xml")
def xml = new groovy.xml.MarkupBuilder(fileOut)
xml.addressBook{
  use(SmartCsvParser){
    fileIn.eachLine{ line ->
      def fields = line.smartSplit()
      entry(id:fields[0]){
        name(fields[1])
        addresss(fields[2])
        city(fields[3])
        state(fields[4])
        zipcode(fields[5])
      }
    }
  }
}

class SmartCsvParser{
  static String[] smartSplit(String self){
    def list = []
    def st = new StringTokenizer(self, ",")
    while(st.hasMoreTokens()){
      def thisToken = st.nextToken()
      while(thisToken.startsWith("\"") && !thisToken.endsWith("\"") ){
        thisToken += "," + st.nextToken()
      }
      list << thisToken.noQuote()
    }
    return list
  }

  static String noQuote(String self){
    if(self.startsWith("\"") || self.startsWith("\'")){
      return self[1..-2]
    }
    else{
      return self
    }
  }
}
```

Let's explore SmartCsvParser in the previous example. smartSplit looks at each token. If the token starts with a double quote and doesn't end with a double quote, you must have a partial field on your hands. smartSplit will continue adding tokens together until it finds the closing quote. Once the fields are all properly joined together, the noQuote method simply strips the surrounding quotes from the field value if necessary.

You used a category (as discussed in Section 10.10, *Adding Methods to a Class Dynamically (Categories)*, on page 188) to add the smartSplit method to the string returned from fileIn.eachLine. This allowed you to keep smartSplit local. If you thought this method was of more global interest, you most likely would have used the ExpandoMetaClass class instead (as discussed in Section 10.11, *Adding Methods to a Class Dynamically (ExpandoMetaClass)*, on page 190).

8.15 Converting JDBC ResultSets to XML

```
//table addressbook:
|name         |address         |city   |st |zipcode
+------------+----------------+-------+---+-------
|John Smith   |456 Fleet St    |Denver |CO |80021
|Jane Doe     |123 Main St     |Denver |CO |80020
|Frank Jones  |345 Center Blvd |Omaha  |NE |68124

//groovy:
def sql = groovy.sql.Sql.newInstance(
  "jdbc:derby://localhost:1527/MyDbTest;create=true",
  "testUser",
  "testPassword",
  "org.apache.derby.jdbc.ClientDriver")

def xml = new groovy.xml.MarkupBuilder()
xml.addressBook{
  sql.eachRow("select * from addressbook"){ row ->
    entry{
      name(row.name)
      addresss(row.address)
      city(row.city)
      state(row.st)
      zipcode(row.zipcode)
    }
  }
}
```

Much like File.eachFile allows you to iterate over every file in a directory (Section 6.1, *Listing All Files in a Directory*, on page 91) and List.each allows you to iterate over every item in a List (Section 3.14, *List Shortcuts*, on page 48), a groovy.sql.Sql object allows you to iterate over a JDBC ResultSet using an eachRow closure. Mixing in a MarkupBuilder gives you a transparent JDBC-to-XML converter.

Chapter 9

Web Services

Web services are everywhere these days. Once we as an industry figured out that XML travels over HTTP as well as HTML, we entered a new age of service-oriented architecture (SOA). This new way of grabbing data from remote sources means that developers must understand the mechanics of low-level TCP/IP and HTTP as well as the various higher-level XML dialects out in the wild: SOAP, REST, and XML-RPC. Luckily, Groovy helps us on all fronts.

In this chapter, we'll start with the low-level basics of how to determine your local TCP/IP address and domain name and those of remote systems. We'll move up the stack to HTTP—learning how to GET, POST, PUT, and DELETE programmatically. We'll end the chapter with examples of how to send and receive SOAP messages, XML-RPC messages, and RESTful requests. We'll even parse a bit of comma-separated value (CSV) data just for old-times' sake.

9.1 Finding Your Local IP Address and Name

```
InetAddress.localHost.hostAddress
===> 63.246.7.76

InetAddress.localHost.hostName
===> myServer

InetAddress.localHost.canonicalHostName
===> www.aboutgroovy.com
```

Before you can communicate with anyone else, it always helps knowing about yourself. In this example, you'll discover your IP address, your local host name, and the DNS name by which the rest of the world knows you.

The InetAddress class comes to you from the java.net package. You cannot directly instantiate an InetAddress class (def addr = new InetAddress()) because the constructor is private. You can, however, use a couple of different static methods to return a well-formed InetAddress. The getLocalHost() method for getting local information is discussed here; getByName() and getAllByName() for getting remote information are discussed in Section 9.2, *Finding a Remote IP Address and Domain Name*, on the next page.

The getLocalHost() method returns an InetAddress that represents the localhost or the hardware on which it is running. As discussed in Section 4.2, *Getter and Setter Shortcut Syntax*, on page 62, getLocalHost() can be shortened to localHost in Groovy. Once you have a handle to localHost, you can call getHostAddress() to get your IP address or getHostName() to get the local machine name. This name is the private name of the system, as opposed to the name registered in DNS for the rest of the world to see. Calling getCanonicalHostName() performs a DNS lookup.

Of course, as discussed in Section 5.4, *Running a Shell Command*, on page 80, the usual command-line tools that ship with your operating system are just an execute() away. They might not be as easy to parse as the InetAddress methods, but as you can see they expose quite a bit more detail.

```
// available on all operating systems
"hostname".execute().text
===> myServer

// on Unix/Linux/Mac OS X
println "ifconfig".execute().text
===>
en2: flags=8963<UP,BROADCAST,SMART,RUNNING,PROMISC,SIMPLEX,MULTICAST> mtu 1500
        inet6 fe80::21c:42ff:fe00:0%en2 prefixlen 64 scopeid 0x8
        inet 10.37.129.3 netmask 0xffffff00 broadcast 10.37.129.255
        ether 00:1c:42:00:00:00
        media: autoselect status: active
        supported media: autoselect

// on Windows
println "ipconfig /all".execute().text
===>
Windows IP Configuration
        Host Name . . . . . . . . . . . . : scottdavis1079
        Primary Dns Suffix  . . . . . . . :
        Node Type . . . . . . . . . . . . : Unknown
        IP Routing Enabled. . . . . . . . : No
        WINS Proxy Enabled. . . . . . . . : No
```

```
Ethernet adapter Local Area Connection:
        Connection-specific DNS Suffix  . :
        Description . . . . . . . . . . : Parallels Network Adapter
        Physical Address. . . . . . . . : 00-61-20-5C-3B-B9
        Dhcp Enabled. . . . . . . . . . : Yes
        Autoconfiguration Enabled . . . . : Yes
        IP Address. . . . . . . . . . . : 10.211.55.3
        Subnet Mask . . . . . . . . . . : 255.255.255.0
        Default Gateway . . . . . . . . : 10.211.55.1
        DHCP Server . . . . . . . . . . : 10.211.55.1
        DNS Servers . . . . . . . . . . : 10.211.55.1
        Lease Obtained. . . . . . . . . : Tuesday, October 09, 2007 2:53:02 PM
        Lease Expires . . . . . . . . . : Tuesday, October 16, 2007 2:53:02 PM
```

9.2 Finding a Remote IP Address and Domain Name

```
InetAddress.getByName("www.aboutgroovy.com")
===> www.aboutgroovy.com/63.246.7.76

InetAddress.getAllByName("www.google.com").each{println it}
===>
www.google.com/64.233.167.99
www.google.com/64.233.167.104
www.google.com/64.233.167.147

InetAddress.getByName("www.google.com").hostAddress
===> 64.233.167.99

InetAddress.getByName("64.233.167.99").canonicalHostName
===> py-in-f99.google.com
```

In addition to its returning information about the local machine, you can use InetAddress to find out about remote systems. getByName() returns a well-formed InetAddress object that represents the remote system. getByName() accepts either a domain name (for example, www.aboutgroovy.com) or an IP address (for example, 64.233.167.99). Once you have a handle to the system, you can ask for its hostAddress and its canonicalHostName.

Sometimes a DNS name can resolve to many different IP addresses. This is especially true for busy websites that load balance the traffic among many physical servers. If a DNS name resolves to more than one IP address, getByName() will return the first one in the list, whereas getAllByName() will return all of them.

Of course, the usual command-line tools for asking about remote systems are available to you as well:

```
// on Unix/Linux/Mac OS X
println "dig www.aboutgroovy.com".execute().text
===>
; <<>> DiG 9.3.4 <<>> www.aboutgroovy.com
;; global options:  printcmd
;; Got answer:
;; ->>HEADER<<- opcode: QUERY, status: NOERROR, id: 55649
;; flags: qr rd ra; QUERY: 1, ANSWER: 1, AUTHORITY: 2, ADDITIONAL: 2

;; QUESTION SECTION:
;www.aboutgroovy.com.            IN      A

;; ANSWER SECTION:
www.aboutgroovy.com.    300     IN      A       63.246.7.76

;; AUTHORITY SECTION:
aboutgroovy.com.        82368   IN      NS      ns1.contegix.com.
aboutgroovy.com.        82368   IN      NS      ns2.contegix.com.

;; ADDITIONAL SECTION:
ns1.contegix.com.       11655   IN      A       63.246.7.200
ns2.contegix.com.       11655   IN      A       63.246.22.100

;; Query time: 204 msec
;; SERVER: 66.174.92.14#53(66.174.92.14)
;; WHEN: Tue Oct  9 15:16:16 2007
;; MSG SIZE  rcvd: 130

// on Windows
println "nslookup www.aboutgroovy.com".execute().text
===>
Server:  UnKnown
Address:  10.211.55.1

Name:    www.aboutgroovy.com
Address:  63.246.7.76
```

9.3 Making an HTTP GET Request

```
def page = new URL("http://www.aboutgroovy.com").text
===>
<html><head><title>...

new URL("http://www.aboutgroovy.com").eachLine{line ->
  println line
}
```

```
===>
<html>
<head>
<title>
...
```

The simplest way to get the contents of an HTML page is to call getText()
on the URL. This allows you to store the entire response in a String variable. If the page is too big to do this comfortably, you can also iterate
through the response line by line using eachLine().

Groovy adds a toURL() method to java.lang.String, allowing you to make
identical requests using a slightly more streamlined syntax:

```
"http://www.aboutgroovy.com".toURL().text
"http://www.aboutgroovy.com".toURL().eachLine{...}
```

We'll discuss how to streamline this to the point where you can simply
call "http://www.aboutgroovy.com".get() in Section 10.11, *Adding Methods
to a Class Dynamically (ExpandoMetaClass)*, on page 190.

Processing a Request Based on the HTTP Response Code

```
def url = new URL("http://www.aboutgroovy.com")
def connection = url.openConnection()
if(connection.responseCode == 200){
  println connection.content.text
}
else{
  println "An error occurred:"
  println connection.responseCode
  println connection.responseMessage
}
```

Calling getText() directly on the URL object means that you expect everything to go perfectly—no connection timeouts, no 404s, and so on.
Although you should be commended on your optimism, if you want
to write slightly more fault-tolerant code, then you should call open-
Connection() on the URL.

This returns a java.net.URLConnection object that will allow you to do
a bit more detailed work with the URL object. connection.content.text
returns the same information as url.text while allowing you to do more
introspection on the response—connection.responseCode for the 200 or
the 404; connection.responseMessage for OK or File Not Found.

Getting HTTP Response Metadata

```
def url = new URL("http://www.aboutgroovy.com")
def connection = url.openConnection()
connection.responseCode
===> 200
connection.responseMessage
===> OK
connection.contentLength
===> 4216
connection.contentType
===> text/html
connection.date
===> 1191250061000
connection.expiration
===> 0
connection.lastModified
===> 0

connection.headerFields.each{println it}
===>
Content-Length=[4216]
Set-Cookie=[JSESSIONID=3B2DE7CBDAE3D58EC46D5A8DF5AF89D1; Path=/]
Date=[Mon, 01 Oct 2007 14:47:41 GMT]
null=[HTTP/1.1 200 OK]
Server=[Apache-Coyote/1.1]
Content-Type=[text/html]
```

Once you have a handle to the URLConnection, you have full access to the accompanying response metadata. In addition to the responseCode and responseMessage, you can ask for things such as the contentLength and the contentType and can even iterate over each response header one by one.

Creating a Convenience GET Class

```
class Get{
  String url
  String queryString
  URLConnection connection
  String text

  String getText(){
    def thisUrl = new URL(this.toString())
    connection = thisUrl.openConnection()
    if(connection.responseCode == 200){
      return connection.content.text
    }
    else{
      return "Something bad happened\n" +
        "URL: " + this.toString() + "\n" +
```

```
            connection.responseCode + ": " +
            connection.responseMessage
      }
   }

   String toString(){
      return url + "?" + queryString
   }
}

def get = new Get(url:"http://search.yahoo.com/search")
get.queryString = "p=groovy"
println get
===> http://search.yahoo.com/search?p=groovy

println get.text
===> <html><head>...

get.url = "http://www.yahoo.com/no.such.page"
println get.text
===>
Something bad happened
URL: http://www.yahoo.com/no.such.page?p=groovy
404: Not Found
```

Up to this point you've been writing some pretty procedural[1] code. It certainly gets the job done, but it suffers just a wee bit in terms of lack of reusability. (Don't you dare suggest that "copy and paste" is a valid type of reuse. You're a good object-oriented programmer—how could you even think such a thing?) This custom Get class wraps everything you've learned up to this point into something that can be reused. It has a nice simple interface and hides enough of the HttpConnection complexity to make it worth your time.

Now, nothing can compare to the simplicity of "http://www.aboutgroovy.com".toURL().text. On the opposite end of the spectrum is Jakarta Commons HttpClient[2]—a great library that is far more complete than anything I could put together on my own. The drawback, of course, is adding yet another dependency to the project. The custom Get class splits the difference nicely. It is slightly more robust than "".toURL().text, and yet it is implemented in pure Groovy so you don't have to worry about JAR bloat in your classpath.

---

1. http://en.wikipedia.org/wiki/Procedural_programming
2. http://jakarta.apache.org/httpcomponents/httpcomponents-client

One more thing: the Get class adds support for a query string. This is a collection of name/value pairs that can be appended to the end of a URL to further customize it. See Section 9.4, *Working with Query Strings* for more information.

RESTful GET Requests

```
"http://search.yahooapis.com/WebSearchService/V1/webSearch?
  appid=YahooDemo&query=groovy&results=10".toURL().text

//alternately, using our Get class
def get = new Get()
get.url = "http://search.yahooapis.com/WebSearchService/V1/webSearch"
get.queryString = "appid=YahooDemo&query=groovy&results=10"
def results = get.text
```

RESTful web services are a type of web service. REST stands for Representational State Transfer.[3] Although there are many differing interpretations of what it means to be truly RESTful, it is generally accepted that an HTTP GET request that returns XML results (as opposed to HTML or some other data format) constitutes the simplest form of a RESTful web service.

Yahoo offers a RESTful API[4] that returns query results in XML. This query returns the top-ten hits for the search term *groovy*. For the result of this query and how to parse it, see Section 9.12, *Parsing Yahoo Search Results as XML*, on page 167.

9.4 Working with Query Strings

```
"http://search.yahoo.com/search?p=groovy".toURL().text
```

A query string allows you to make more complex HTTP GET requests by adding name/value pairs to the end of the address. Now instead of just asking for a static page at http://search.yahoo.com, you can make a dynamic query for all pages that contain the word *groovy*.

The Web is transformed from a simple distributed filesystem to a fully programmable Web.[5] The mechanics of programmatically making an HTTP GET request don't change—it is no more complicated than what we discussed in Section 9.3, *Making an HTTP GET Request*, on page 146.

---

3. http://en.wikipedia.org/wiki/Representational_State_Transfer
4. http://developer.yahoo.com/search/web/V1/webSearch.html
5. http://www.programmableweb.com/

However, the semantics of using query strings opens up a whole new world of programmatic possibilities.

For example, complicated web pages like a Google map showing the Denver International Airport can be captured in a single URL. This means we can hyperlink it, bookmark it, or email it to a friend simply by clicking Link to This Page in the upper-right corner of the page. Each element in the query string represents a different aspect of the map: ll for the latitude/longitude center point of the map (39.87075,-104.694214), z for the zoom level (11), t for the type (h, or hybrid), and so forth.

```
"http://maps.google.com/maps?f=q&hl=en&geocode=&time=&date=&ttype=
&q=dia&sll=37.0625,-95.677068&sspn=34.038806,73.125&ie=UTF8
&ll=39.87075,-104.694214&spn=0.2577,0.571289&z=11&iwloc=addr&om=1&t=h"
.toURL().text
```

Building the Query String from a List

```
def queryString = []
queryString << "n=" + URLEncoder.encode("20")
queryString << "vd=" + URLEncoder.encode("m3")
queryString << "vl=" + URLEncoder.encode("lang_en")
queryString << "vf=" + URLEncoder.encode("pdf")
queryString << "p=" + URLEncoder.encode("groovy grails")

def address = "http://search.yahoo.com/search"
def url = new URL(address + "?" + queryString.join("&"))
println url
===>
http://search.yahoo.com/search?n=20&vd=m3&vl=lang_en&vf=pdf&p=groovy+grails

println url.text
```

Often you'll be tasked with assembling a well-formed query string from an arbitrary collection of data values. The secret is to make sure the values are URL encoded[6] ("foo bar baz" ==> foo+bar+baz), while the name portion (nonsense=) remains plain text. If you try to URL encode the name and the value as a single string ("nonsense=foo bar baz"), the equals sign (=) will get converted to %3D, and your web server will most likely reject the request.

This example creates a List of name/value pairs, ensuring that only the value gets URL encoded using the java.net.URLEncoder. Later when you need the well-formed query string, you call queryString.join("&"). As we

---

6. http://en.wikipedia.org/wiki/Urlencode

discussed in Section 3.14, *Join*, on page 50, this returns the list as a single string with each element joined by the string you passed in as the parameter.

This particular query string was built by performing an advanced Yahoo search and cherry-picking the interesting name/value pairs from the resulting URL. n returns twenty results instead of the default ten. vd limits the results to those posted in the past three months. vl returns only English pages. vf filters the results for only PDF documents. And finally, p looks for results that mention either *groovy* or *grails*.

Building the Query String from a Map

```
def map = [n:20, vf:"pdf", p:"groovy grails"]
def list = []
map.each{name,value->
  list << "$name=" + URLEncoder.encode(value.toString())
}
println list.join("&")
===> n=20&vf=pdf&p=groovy+grails
```

Groovy Maps are a great way to represent query strings since both naturally have name/value pairs. This example still uses a temporary List to store the URL-encoded values and a join("&") to put them together at the last minute.

There is one edge case that keeps this from being a 100% solution. Query strings are allowed to have duplicate named elements, whereas Maps enforce unique names.

```
http://localhost/order?book=Groovy+Recipes&book=Groovy+In+Action
```

If you can live with this limitation, then Maps are the perfect solution. If you need to support duplicate named elements, see Section 9.4, *Creating a Convenience QueryString Class* for more information.

Creating a Convenience QueryString Class

```
class QueryString{
  Map params = [:]

  //this constructor allows you to pass in a Map
  QueryString(Map params){
    if(params){
      this.params.putAll(params)
    }
  }
}
```

```
  //this method allows you to add name/value pairs
  void add(String name, Object value){
    params.put(name, value)
  }

  //this method returns a well-formed QueryString
  String toString(){
    def list = []
    params.each{name,value->
      list << "$name=" + URLEncoder.encode(value.toString())
    }
    return list.join("&")
  }
}

def qs = new QueryString(n:20, vf:"pdf", p:"groovy grails")
println qs
===> n=20&vf=pdf&p=groovy+grails

def qs2 = new QueryString()
qs2.params.put("firstname", "Scott")
qs2.add("id", 99)
qs2.add "updated", new Date()
println qs2
===> firstname=Scott&id=99&updated=Wed+Oct+10+20%3A17%3A34+MDT+2007
```

Creating a convenience class allows you to encapsulate the mechanics of building a well-formed query string into a reusable component.

The qs object accepts name/value pairs in the constructor that get coerced into a Map. (You could have also passed in an existing Map to the constructor.) The qs2 object demonstrates three different ways to pass in name/values pairs—by accessing the params Map directly, by using the convenient add() method with parentheses, and finally by calling the same add() method while taking advantage of Groovy's optional parentheses.

Notice that the add() method accepts an Object for the value. This allows you to store values such as integers and classes instead of simple strings. Calling URLEncoder.encode(value.toString()) ensures that the values get plugged into the query string correctly.

Combining the query string with the Get class created in Section 9.3, *Creating a Convenience GET Class*, on page 148 begins to demonstrate the power you've managed to assemble with very little code—there are fewer than fifty lines of code between Get and QueryString.

```groovy
class Get{
  String url
  QueryString queryString = new QueryString()
  URLConnection connection
  String text

  String getText(){
    def thisUrl = new URL(this.toString())
    connection = thisUrl.openConnection()
    if(connection.responseCode == 200){
      return connection.content.text
    } else{
      return "Something bad happened\n" +
        "URL: " + this.toString() + "\n" +
        connection.responseCode + ": " +
        connection.responseMessage
    }
  }

  String toString(){
    return url + "?" + queryString.toString()
  }
}
def get = new Get(url:"http://search.yahoo.com/search")
get.queryString.add("n", 20)
get.queryString.add("vf", "pdf")
get.queryString.add("p", "groovy grails")

println get
===> http://search.yahoo.com/search?n=20&vf=pdf&p=groovy+grails

println get.text
===> <html><head>...
```

Notice that upgrading your queryString field from a String to a full-fledged QueryString object requires touching the Get class in only two places. The field declaration now creates a new QueryString(), and the toString() method calls queryString.toString(). This upgrade now allows you to let the Get class create the well-formed QueryString instead of forcing you to create one on your own. Calls such as get.queryString.add("p", "groovy grails") do the right thing behind the scenes, ensuring that the values are properly URL encoded.

Remember the query string/hashmap mismatch we discussed in Section 9.4, *Building the Query String from a Map*, on page 152? Because the QueryString class is currently implemented, each call to qs.add() replaces the name/value pair. To support duplicate named elements, the QueryString class would need to be refactored to append values to a List if the name existed. For an idea of how to add this feature, see Section 10.8, *Calling Methods That Don't Exist (invokeMethod)*, on page 185.

9.5 Making an HTTP POST Request

```
def url = new URL("http://search.yahoo.com/search")
def connection = url.openConnection()

//switch the method to POST (GET is the default)
connection.setRequestMethod("POST")

//write the data
def queryString = "n=20&vf=pdf&p=groovy+grails"
connection.doOutput = true
Writer writer = new OutputStreamWriter(connection.outputStream)
writer.write(queryString)
writer.flush()
writer.close()
connection.connect()

//print the results
println connection.content.text
===> <html><head>...
```

When making an HTTP POST request, you cannot use the same get-Text() shortcut on the URL class that you could when making a GET request. You must get the URLConnection so that you can set the request method to POST (GET is the default). For a GET request, the query string is appended to the end of the URL object. In contrast, the query string of a POST is embedded in the body of the request. To accomplish this, you must do three things: set the doOutput value of the URLConnection to true, get the outputStream, and write the query string to it before you call connect().

Building the Query String from a List

```
def queryString = []
queryString << "n=" + URLEncoder.encode("20")
queryString << "vf=" + URLEncoder.encode("pdf")
queryString << "p=" + URLEncoder.encode("groovy grails")

def url = new URL("http://search.yahoo.com/search")
def connection = url.openConnection()
connection.setRequestMethod("POST")
connection.doOutput = true
Writer writer = new OutputStreamWriter(connection.outputStream)
writer.write(queryString.join("&"))
writer.flush()
writer.close()
connection.connect()

def results = conn.content.text
```

As discussed in Section 9.4, *Building the Query String from a List*, on page 151, the secret to building up a query string from a List is making sure the values get URL encoded and then joining the elements together with an &.

Creating a Convenience Post Class

```
class Post{
  String url
  QueryString queryString = new QueryString()
  URLConnection connection
  String text

  String getText(){
    def thisUrl = new URL(url)
    connection = thisUrl.openConnection()
    connection.setRequestMethod("POST")
    connection.doOutput = true
    Writer writer = new OutputStreamWriter(connection.outputStream)
    writer.write(queryString.toString())
    writer.flush()
    writer.close()
    connection.connect()
    return connection.content.text
  }

  String toString(){
    return "POST:\n" +
      url + "\n" +
      queryString.toString()
  }
}

def post = new Post(url:"http://search.yahoo.com/search")
post.queryString.add("n", 20)
post.queryString.add("vf", "pdf")
post.queryString.add("p", "groovy grails")

println post
===>
POST:
http://search.yahoo.com/search
n=20&vf=pdf&p=groovy+grails

println post.text
===> <html><head>...
```

Putting all the complicated connection logic into a Post class—combined with the QueryString class you created in Section 9.4, *Creating a Convenience QueryString Class*, on page 152—makes for a pretty compelling development experience.

Mocking HTML Forms for Testing

```
<form method="post" action="http://localhost:8888/jaw/controller">
  <input type="hidden" name="action" value="saveCar" />
  Make:  <input type="text" name="make" value="" /></td>
  Model: <input type="text" name="model" value="" /></td>
  Year:  <input type="text" name="modelYear" value="" /></td>
  <input type="submit" name="save" value="Save" />
</form>
```

Now that you have Post class, you can easily mock up an HTML form submission using code. Given this HTML form, you could simulate a user filling out the form and clicking the submit button using the following code:

```
def post = new Post(url:"http://localhost:8888/jaw/controller")
post.queryString.add("action", "saveCar")
post.queryString.add("make", "Toyota")
post.queryString.add("model", "Prius")
post.queryString.add("modelYear", 2012)
println post.text
```

All that is left to do at this point is to write the assertion on post.text that verifies the form submission was performed correctly.

RESTful POST Requests Using XML

```
def xml = """<car>
  <make>Toyota</make>
  <model-year>2012</model-year>
  <model>Prius</model>
</car>"""

def url = new URL("http://localhost:8888/jaw/car")
def connection = url.openConnection()

//set the metadata
connection.setRequestMethod("POST")
connection.setRequestProperty("Content-Type","application/xml")

//write the data
connection.doOutput = true
Writer writer = new OutputStreamWriter(connection.outputStream)
writer.write(xml)
writer.flush()
writer.close()
connection.connect()

def results = connection.content.text
```

In RESTful web services, the HTTP verb used for the request has deep semantic meaning. A common database metaphor—create, retrieve, update, delete (CRUD)—is equally applicable to RESTful applications,[7] although the verbs used in SQL statements aren't identical. The SELECT you perform against a database is analogous to an HTTP GET. You INSERT records into a table, whereas you POST form data to a website. HTTP PUT is the equivalent of a database UPDATE. DELETE is the least surprising of all—it has the same meaning in both SQL and HTTP.

RESTful web services usually expect XML in the body of the POST as opposed to the query strings being demonstrated up to this point. To pass in XML, you need to make two minor changes to your code. First, you'll most likely need to change the Content-Type from application/x-www-form-urlencoded (the default for POST) to application/xml. (The exact Content-Type depends on the RESTful service you are calling.) The other thing you need to do is *not* URL encode the data. The XML payload should be transported in its native format. For another example of POSTing XML, see Section 9.10, *Making a SOAP Request*, on page 163.

9.6 Making an HTTP PUT Request

```
def xml = """<car id="142">
  <make>Toyota</make>
  <model-year>2012</model-year>
  <model>Prius, Luxury Edition</model>
</car>"""

def url = new URL("http://localhost:8888/jaw/car/142")
def connection = url.openConnection()
connection.setRequestMethod("PUT")
connection.setRequestProperty("Content-Type","application/xml")
connection.doOutput = true
Writer writer = new OutputStreamWriter(connection.outputStream)
writer.write(xml)
writer.flush()
writer.close()
connection.connect()

def result = connection.content.text
```

Performing an HTTP PUT is syntactically identical to performing a POST with one exception—connection.setRequestMethod("PUT"). As discussed in Section 9.5, *RESTful POST Requests Using XML*, on the preceding page, a PUT is semantically an UPDATE, whereas a POST is equivalent to a SQL INSERT. This example updates the model description to include "Luxury Edition."

---

7. http://en.wikipedia.org/wiki/Create\%2C_read\%2C_update_and_delete

Creating a Convenience Put Class

```
class Put{
  String url
  String body
  String contentType = "application/xml"
  URLConnection connection
  String text

  String getText(){
    def thisUrl = new URL(url)
    connection = thisUrl.openConnection()
    connection.setRequestMethod("PUT")
    connection.setRequestProperty("Content-Type", contentType)
    connection.doOutput = true
    Writer writer = new OutputStreamWriter(connection.outputStream)
    writer.write(body)
    writer.flush()
    writer.close()
    connection.connect()
    return connection.content.text
  }

  String toString(){
    return "PUT:\n" +
      contentType + "\n" +
      url + "\n" +
      body
  }
}

def xml = """<car id="142">
  <make>Toyota</make>
  <model-year>2012</model-year>
  <model>Prius, Luxury Edition</model>
</car>"""

def put = new Put(url:"http://localhost:8888/jaw/car/142")
put.body = xml
println put
===>
PUT:
application/xml
http://localhost:8888/jaw/car/142
<car id="142">
  <make>Toyota</make>
  <model-year>2012</model-year>
  <model>Prius, Luxury Edition</model>
</car>

def result = put.text
```

The Put class is almost identical to the Post class with three distinctions.

The queryString field is exchanged for a plain old Stringbody field. Also, you expose a contentType field so that you can change it as needed. Finally, the requestMethod is set to PUT.

9.7 Making an HTTP DELETE Request

```
def url = new URL("http://localhost:8888/jaw/car/142")
def connection = url.openConnection()
connection.setRequestMethod("DELETE")
connection.connect()

def result = connection.content.text
```

Performing an HTTP DELETE is syntactically identical to performing a GET with one exception—connection.setRequestMethod("DELETE"). Whereas POST and PUT requests have data in the body, GET and DELETE (as well as HEAD, OPTION, and the rest of the HTTP verbs) have only a URL. As discussed in Section 9.5, *RESTful POST Requests Using XML*, on page 157, a DELETE does exactly what you'd expect it to do—effectively delete from cars where id=142.

Creating a Convenience Delete Class

```
class Delete{
  String url
  QueryString queryString = new QueryString()
  URLConnection connection
  String text

  String getText(){
    def thisUrl = new URL(this.toString())
    connection = thisUrl.openConnection()
        connection.setRequestMethod("DELETE")
    if(connection.responseCode == 200){
      return connection.content.text
    }
    else{
      return "Something bad happened\n" +
        "URL: " + this.toString() + "\n" +
        connection.responseCode + ": " +
        connection.responseMessage
    }
  }

  String toString(){
    return "DELETE:\n" +
    url + "?" + queryString.toString()
  }
}
```

```
def delete = new Delete(url:"http://localhost:8888/jaw/car/142")
println delete
===>
DELETE:
http://localhost:8888/jaw/car/142

def results = delete.text
```

The Delete class is almost identical to the Get class with one distinction: requestMethod is set to DELETE.

9.8 Making a RESTful Request

```
def partialRestRequest = "http://geocoder.us/service/rest/geocode?address="
def address = "1600 Pennsylvania Ave, Washington DC"
def restUrl = new URL(partialRestRequest + URLEncoder.encode(address))
def restResponse = restUrl.text
```

This request returns the latitude/longitude for the White House as XML. Feel free to substitute your own address. You can see the returned point on a map by visiting http://geocoder.us or by typing the coordinate pair into the search box of any of the major mapping websites.

Parsing a RESTful Response

```
//Response:
<rdf:RDF
  xmlns:dc="http://purl.org/dc/elements/1.1/"
  xmlns:geo="http://www.w3.org/2003/01/geo/wgs84_pos#"
  xmlns:rdf="http://www.w3.org/1999/02/22-rdf-syntax-ns#">
  <geo:Point rdf:nodeID="aid76408515">
    <dc:description>
      1600 Pennsylvania Ave NW, Washington DC 20502
    </dc:description>
    <geo:long>-77.037684</geo:long>
    <geo:lat>38.898748</geo:lat>
  </geo:Point>
</rdf:RDF>

def restResponse = restUrl.text
def RDF = new XmlSlurper().parseText(restResponse)
println RDF.Point.description
println RDF.Point.long
println RDF.Point.lat
```

XmlSlurper allows you to avoid dealing with the namespaces and extract the pertinent fields. See Section 7.9, *Parsing an XML Document with Namespaces*, on page 123 for more information.

Web Services Case Study: Geocoder.us

If you've ever used Google Maps,* Yahoo! Maps,† MapQuest,‡ Microsoft Live Search,§ or any of the other mapping websites, you've been using web services without even realizing it. The address you type into the site—123 Main St., for example—is not inherently mappable. To plot the address on the map, the street address must be converted into a latitude/longitude point. The type of web service that does this sort of conversion is called a *geocoder*.

All of the major mapping websites offer geocoding APIs, but there is an independent geocoding website that plays a prominent role in several of the examples in this chapter. Geocoder.us¶ works well as fodder for Section 9.8, *Making a RESTful Request*, on the preceding page; Section 9.9, *Making a CSV Request*, on the next page; Section 9.10, *Making a SOAP Request*, on the facing page; and Section 9.11, *Making an XML-RPC Request*, on page 165. That's because it allows you to make the same basic query in a variety of different web service dialects. Geocoder.us is a free service for noncommercial use based on free data from the U.S. Census Bureau.

There are a few other formats that Geocoder.us doesn't support at the time of this writing—RSS and Atom. You can reach out to AboutGroovy.com for real-world examples of them, but don't be surprised if Geocoder.us adds these formats into the mix at some point. GeoRSS and GeoAtom both exist and are gaining popularity. Flickr,‖ for example, offers a GeoRSS feed at the bottom of every search results page.

---

*.   http://maps.google.com
†.   http://maps.yahoo.com
‡.   http://www.mapquest.com
§.   http://maps.live.com/
¶.   http://geocoder.us
‖.   http://flickr.com

9.9 Making a CSV Request

```
def partialCsvRequest = "http://geocoder.us/service/csv/geocode?address="
def address = "1600 Pennsylvania Ave, Washington DC"
def csvUrl = new URL(partialCsvRequest + URLEncoder.encode(address))
def csvResponse = csvUrl.text
```

This request returns the latitude/longitude for the White House as CSV. Feel free to substitute your own address. You can see the returned point on a map by visiting http://geocoder.us or by typing the coordinate pair into the search box of any of the major mapping websites.

Parsing a CSV Response

```
//Response:
38.898748,-77.037684,1600 Pennsylvania Ave NW,Washington,DC,20502

def csvResponse = csvUrl.text
def tokens = csvResponse.split(",")
println "Latitude:   [${tokens[0]}]"
println "Longitude:  [${tokens[1]}]"
println "Address:    [${tokens[2]}]"
println "City:       [${tokens[3]}]"
println "State:      [${tokens[4]}]"
println "Zip:        [${tokens[5]}]"
```

Calling split(",") on the result string allows you to easily get at the individual fields. For more information on parsing CSV, see Section 8.14, *Converting CSV to XML*, on page 139.

9.10 Making a SOAP Request

```
def address = "1600 Pennsylvania Av, Washington, DC"
def soapRequest = """<SOAP-ENV:Envelope
  xmlns:SOAP-ENV="http://schemas.xmlsoap.org/soap/envelope/"
  xmlns:xsi="http://www.w3.org/1999/XMLSchema-instance"
  xmlns:xsd="http://www.w3.org/1999/XMLSchema"
  xmlns:tns="http://rpc.geocoder.us/Geo/Coder/US/">
  <SOAP-ENV:Body>
    <tns:geocode
        SOAP-ENV:encodingStyle="http://schemas.xmlsoap.org/soap/encoding/">
      <location xsi:type="xsd:string">${address}</location>
    </tns:geocode>
  </SOAP-ENV:Body>
</SOAP-ENV:Envelope>"""

def soapUrl = new URL("http://geocoder.us/service/soap")
def connection = soapUrl.openConnection()
connection.setRequestMethod("POST")
connection.setRequestProperty("Content-Type","application/xml")
connection.doOutput = true
```

```
Writer writer = new OutputStreamWriter(connection.outputStream)
writer.write(soapRequest)
writer.flush()
writer.close()
connection.connect()

def soapResponse = connection.content.text
```

This returns the latitude/longitude for the White House as SOAP. Feel
free to substitute your own address. You can see the returned point on
a map by visiting http://geocoder.us or by typing the coordinate pair into
the search box of any of the major mapping websites.

What you're seeing here is the way to make the raw SOAP request
by POSTing the SOAP envelope directly. You can find the WSDL document for this service at http://geocoder.us/dist/eg/clients/GeoCoder.wsdl.
Once you have the WSDL, you can always use any of the standard
wsdl2java/java2wsdl utilities that ship with most SOAP frameworks.

Parsing a SOAP Response

```
//Response:
<?xml version="1.0" encoding="utf-8"?>
<SOAP-ENV:Envelope xmlns:xsi="http://www.w3.org/1999/XMLSchema-instance"
xmlns:SOAP-ENC="http://schemas.xmlsoap.org/soap/encoding/"
xmlns:SOAP-ENV="http://schemas.xmlsoap.org/soap/envelope/"
xmlns:xsd="http://www.w3.org/1999/XMLSchema"
SOAP-ENV:encodingStyle="http://schemas.xmlsoap.org/soap/encoding/">
  <SOAP-ENV:Body>
    <namesp9:geocodeResponse
      xmlns:namesp9="http://rpc.geocoder.us/Geo/Coder/US/">
      <geo:s-gensym111 xsi:type="SOAP-ENC:Array"
      xmlns:geo="http://rpc.geocoder.us/Geo/Coder/US/"
      SOAP-ENC:arrayType="geo:GeocoderAddressResult[1]">
        <item xsi:type="geo:GeocoderAddressResult">
          <number xsi:type="xsd:int">1600</number>
          <lat xsi:type="xsd:float">38.898748</lat>
          <street xsi:type="xsd:string">Pennsylvania</street>
          <state xsi:type="xsd:string">DC</state>
          <city xsi:type="xsd:string">Washington</city>
          <zip xsi:type="xsd:int">20502</zip>
          <suffix xsi:type="xsd:string">NW</suffix>
          <long xsi:type="xsd:float">-77.037684</long>
          <type xsi:type="xsd:string">Ave</type>
          <prefix xsi:type="xsd:string" />
        </item>
      </geo:s-gensym111>
    </namesp9:geocodeResponse>
  </SOAP-ENV:Body>
</SOAP-ENV:Envelope>
```

```
def soapResponse = connection.content.text
def Envelope = new XmlSlurper().parseText(soapResponse)
println Envelope.Body.geocodeResponse.'s-gensym111'.item.long
println Envelope.Body.geocodeResponse.'s-gensym111'.item.lat

//since the array's name ('s-gensym111') changes with each request
// we can deal with it generically as such:
def itor = Envelope.Body.geocodeResponse.breadthFirst()
while(itor.hasNext()){
  def fragment = itor.next()
  if(fragment.name() == "item"){
    println fragment.lat
    println fragment.long
  }
}
```

XmlSlurper allows you to avoid dealing with the namespaces and extract the pertinent fields. See Section 7.9, *Parsing an XML Document with Namespaces*, on page 123 for more information.

The SOAP interface to Geocoder.us is a bit atypical. The namespace for geocodeResponse and the element name of the array element inside it both vary from response to response. This makes it impossible to hard-code a GPath to the deeply buried elements lat and long. In every other SOAP-based web service I've dealt with, element names and namespaces are quite stable and rarely change.

Despite the bugs, I decided to stick with this site for the SOAP example. The ability to make the same request to the same service in four different dialects, coupled with the unexpected "bonus" of being able to show how to flexibly work around response oddities, made it too good to pass up. Since I'm trying to show you client-side code rather than a canonical server-side SOAP example, I figured that you'd be able to overlook a bump or two in the road.

9.11 Making an XML-RPC Request

```
def address = "1600 Pennsylvania Av, Washington, DC"
def xmlrpcRequest = """<methodCall>
  <methodName>geocode</methodName>
  <params>
    <param>
        <value><string>${address}</string></value>
    </param>
  </params>
</methodCall>"""
```

```
def xmlrpcUrl = new URL("http://geocoder.us/service/xmlrpc")
def connection = xmlrpcUrl.openConnection()
connection.setRequestMethod("POST")
connection.setRequestProperty("Content-Type","application/xml")
connection.doOutput = true
Writer writer = new OutputStreamWriter(connection.outputStream)
writer.write(xmlrpcRequest)
writer.flush()
writer.close()
connection.connect()

def xmlrpcResponse = connection.content.text
```

This request returns the latitude/longitude for the White House as XML-RPC. Feel free to substitute your own address. You can see the returned point on a map by visiting http://geocoder.us or by typing the coordinate pair into the search box of any of the major mapping websites.

Parsing an XML-RPC Response

```
//Response:
<?xml version="1.0" encoding="UTF-8"?>
<methodResponse><params><param><value><array><data><value><struct>
<member><name>number</name><value><int>1600</int></value></member>
<member><name>lat</name><value><double>38.898748</double></value></member>
<member><name>street</name><value><string>Pennsylvania</string></value></member>
<member><name>state</name><value><string>DC</string></value></member>
<member><name>city</name><value><string>Washington</string></value></member>
<member><name>zip</name><value><int>20502</int></value></member>
<member><name>suffix</name><value><string>NW</string></value></member>
<member><name>long</name><value><double>-77.037684</double></value></member>
<member><name>type</name><value><string>Ave</string></value></member>
<member><name>prefix</name><value><string/></value></member>
</struct></value></data></array></value></param></params></methodResponse>

def xmlrpcResponse = connection.content.text
def methodResponse = new XmlSlurper().parseText(xmlrpcResponse)
methodResponse.params.param.value.array.data.value.struct.member.each{member ->
  if(member.name == "lat" || member.name == "long"){
    println "${member.name}: ${member.value.double}"
  }
}
```

XmlSlurper allows you to avoid dealing with the namespaces and extract the pertinent fields. See Section 7.9, *Parsing an XML Document with Namespaces*, on page 123 for more information. Despite the almost comical depth of the nested response (your target lat and long elements are eleven levels deep), you are able to get at them with ease and print the results.

9.12 Parsing Yahoo Search Results as XML

```
def yahooAddress = "http://search.yahooapis.com/WebSearchService/V1/webSearch?"
def queryString = "appid=YahooDemo&query=groovy&results=10"
def xmlResponse = "${yahooAddress}${queryString}".toURL().text
```

As discussed in Section 9.3, *RESTful GET Requests*, on page 150, Yahoo offers a RESTful API that returns search results as XML instead of the usual HTML. You can adjust the query in a number of different ways by simply tweaking the name/value pairs on the query string.

Parsing XML Yahoo Search Results

```
//Response:
<ResultSet
xmlns:xsi="http://www.w3.org/2001/XMLSchema-instance"
xmlns="urn:yahoo:srch"
xsi:schemaLocation="urn:yahoo:srch
  http://api.search.yahoo.com/WebSearchService/V1/WebSearchResponse.xsd"
type="web"
totalResultsAvailable="20700000"
totalResultsReturned="10"
firstResultPosition="1"
moreSearch="/WebSearchService/V1/webSearch?query=groovy&amp;appid=YahooDemo">
  <Result>
    <Title>Groovy - Home</Title>
    <Summary>Groovy ... </Summary>
    <Url>http://groovy.codehaus.org/</Url>
    <ClickUrl>http://uk.wrs.yahoo.com/</ClickUrl>
    <DisplayUrl>groovy.codehaus.org/</DisplayUrl>
    <ModificationDate>1191394800</ModificationDate>
    <MimeType>text/html</MimeType>
    <Cache><Url>http://uk.wrs.yahoo.com/</Url><Size>39661</Size></Cache>
  </Result>
</ResultSet>

def ResultSet = new XmlSlurper().parseText(xmlResponse)
ResultSet.Result.each{
  println it.Title
  println it.Url
  println "-----"
}
===>
Groovy - Home
http://groovy.codehaus.org/
-----
Groovy - Wikipedia, the free encyclopedia
http://en.wikipedia.org/wiki/Groovy
-----
...
```

XmlSlurper allows you to avoid dealing with the namespaces and extract the pertinent fields. See Section 7.9, *Parsing an XML Document with Namespaces*, on page 123 for more information.

9.13 Parsing an Atom Feed

```
def atom = "http://aboutgroovy.com/item/atom".toURL().text
```

Grabbing the Atom[8] syndication feed for AboutGroovy.com is trivial. Since it is a simple HTTP GET that doesn't even require a query string, it almost seems anticlimactic compared to the heroic steps we had to go through to POST a SOAP request.

```
//Response:
<feed xmlns="http://www.w3.org/2005/Atom">
<title type="text">aboutGroovy.com</title>
<link rel="alternate" type="text/html" href="http://aboutGroovy.com"/>
<link rel="self" type="application/atom+xml"
      href="http://aboutGroovy.com/item/atom" />
<updated>2007-10-10T13:15:23-07:00</updated>
<author><name>Scott Davis</name></author>
<id>tag:aboutgroovy.com,2006-12-18:thisIsUnique</id>
<generator uri="http://aboutGroovy.com" version="0.0.2">
    Hand-rolled Grails code</generator>

  <entry xmlns='http://www.w3.org/2005/Atom'>
    <author><name>Scott Davis</name></author>
    <published>2007-10-10T10:44:48-07:00</published>
    <updated>2007-10-10T10:44:48-07:00</updated>
    <link href='http://aboutGroovy.com/item/show/258'
        rel='alternate'
        title='G2One, Inc. -- Professional Support for Groovy and Grails'
        type='text/html' />
    <id>tag:aboutgroovy.com,2006:/item/show/258</id>
    <title type='text'>
      G2One, Inc. -- Professional Support for Groovy and Grails
    </title>
    <content type='xhtml'>
      <div xmlns='http://www.w3.org/1999/xhtml'>
        <p>Category: news</p>
        <p><a href='http://www.g2one.com/'>Original Source</a></p>
        <p>Groovy and Grails now have a corporate home -- G2One. The project
            leads for both Groovy and Grails (Guillaume Laforge and Graeme
            Rocher) have joined forces with Alex Tkachman (until recently
            with JetBrains) to form a new company.</p>
      </div>
    </content>
  </entry>
</feed>
```

---

8. http://en.wikipedia.org/wiki/Atom_\%28standard\%29

```
def feed = new XmlSlurper().parseText(atom)
feed.entry.each{
  println it.title
  println it.published
  println "-----"
}
```

```
===>
SAP Adds Groovy/Grails Support
2007-10-10T10:52:21-07:00
-----
G2One, Inc. -- Professional Support for Groovy and Grails
2007-10-10T10:44:48-07:00
-----
...
```

XmlSlurper allows you to avoid dealing with the namespaces and extract the pertinent fields. See Section 7.9, *Parsing an XML Document with Namespaces*, on page 123 for more information.

Atom is an implementation of REST that is gaining popularity beyond simple blogosphere syndication. Google officially deprecated its SOAP API in December 2006. It is migrating all of its web services to Atom under the GData[9] initiative. For a well-documented example of a fully RESTful API—one that includes authentication and full CRUD using HTTP GET, POST, PUT, and DELETE—see the Google Calendar API.

For information on how to create an Atom feed, see Section 12.4, *Setting Up an Atom Feed*, on page 233.

9.14 Parsing an RSS Feed

```
def rssFeed = "http://aboutgroovy.com/podcast/rss".toURL().text
```

Getting an RSS feed is as simple as making a plain old HTTP GET request.

```
//Response:
<rss xmlns:itunes="http://www.itunes.com/dtds/podcast-1.0.dtd" version="2.0">
  <channel>
  <title>About Groovy Podcasts</title>
  <link>http://aboutGroovy.com</link>
  <language>en-us</language>
  <copyright>2007 AboutGroovy.com</copyright>
  <itunes:subtitle>
    Your source for the very latest Groovy and Grails news
  </itunes:subtitle>
```

---

9. http://code.google.com/apis/gdata/

```xml
      <itunes:author>Scott Davis</itunes:author>
      <itunes:summary>About Groovy interviews</itunes:summary>
      <description>About Groovy interviews</description>
      <itunes:owner>
        <itunes:name>Scott Davis</itunes:name>
        <itunes:email>scott@aboutGroovy.com</itunes:email>
      </itunes:owner>
      <itunes:image href="http://aboutgroovy.com/images/aboutGroovy3.png" />
      <itunes:category text="Technology" />
      <itunes:category text="Java" />
      <itunes:category text="Groovy" />
      <itunes:category text="Grails" />
      <item>
        <title>AboutGroovy Interviews Neal Ford</title>
        <itunes:author>Scott Davis</itunes:author>
        <itunes:subtitle></itunes:subtitle>
        <itunes:summary>Neal Ford of ThoughtWorks is truly a polyglot programmer.
            In this exclusive interview, Neal opines on Groovy, Ruby, Java, DSLs, and
            the future of programming languages. Opinionated and entertaining, Neal
            doesn't pull any punches. Enjoy.
        </itunes:summary>
        <enclosure url="http://aboutgroovy.com/podcasts/NealFord.mp3"
                   length="33720522" type="audio/mpeg" />
        <guid>http://aboutgroovy.com/podcasts/NealFord.mp3</guid>
        <pubDate>2007-04-17T01:15:00-07:00</pubDate>
        <itunes:duration>44:19</itunes:duration>
        <itunes:keywords>java,groovy,grails</itunes:keywords>
      </item>
  </channel>
</rss>
```

```groovy
def rss = new XmlSlurper().parseText(rssFeed)
rss.channel.item.each{
  println it.title
  println it.pubDate
  println it.enclosure.@url
  println it.duration
  println "-----"
}
```

```
===>
AboutGroovy Interviews Neal Ford
2007-04-17T01:15:00-07:00
http://aboutgroovy.com/podcasts/NealFord.mp3
44:19
-----
AboutGroovy Interviews Jeremy Rayner
2007-03-13T01:18:00-07:00
http://aboutgroovy.com/podcasts/JeremyRayner.mp3
50:54
-----
...
```

XmlSlurper allows you to avoid dealing with the namespaces and extract the pertinent fields. See Section 7.9, *Parsing an XML Document with Namespaces*, on page 123 for more information.

Yahoo has a number of RSS feeds that offer more than simple blog syndication. For a couple of examples of RSS feeds that send real data down the wire, see both http://developer.yahoo.com/weather/ as well as http://developer.yahoo.com/traffic/.

Chapter 10

Metaprogramming

Metaprogramming[1] is writing code that has the ability to dynamically change its behavior at runtime. (I'd like *this* class to have *that* method on it *right now*.) It gives a fluidity and flexibility to your code that can seem positively alien if you are steeped in static programming languages such as C or Java. Dynamic languages such as Smalltalk and Ruby have this capability, and now Groovy allows you to do the same type of thing within a Java environment.

No self-respecting dynamic language would be complete without the complementary idea of *reflection*[2]—the ability to programmatically ask itself about itself at runtime. (What fields does this class have? What methods will it respond to?) Although this is *possible* in Java by using the Reflection API, in practice it is rarely used. Some might argue that the concepts are less relevant in a statically typed language than a dynamically typed one—after all, once you define an interface in Java, why programmatically ask the interface which methods it defines? You already know the answer to the question *a priori*, and in Java the interface will never change. (Polymorphism is based on this concept.)

In Chapter 3, *New to Groovy*, on page 31, we discussed interesting add-ons to the Java language. Most developers already know what a java.util.ArrayList is, so pointing out the additional cool new methods is an exercise in working with a familiar class in a new way. Unless you've already been working with the Reflection API in Java or habitually instantiating all of your classes via Class.forName(), the ideas in this

---

1. http://en.wikipedia.org/wiki/Metaprogramming
2. http://en.wikipedia.org/wiki/Reflection_\%28computer_science\%29

chapter might be a bit of a stretch in a new direction. (Why should you programmatically ask this class if it has a field or responds to a specific method—isn't that what your compiler does for you?)

This chapter shows you ways to programmatically ask your class what fields and methods it has. We'll also look at how to dynamically add new fields and methods at runtime via the MetaClass class. We'll talk about calling methods that don't exist using invokeMethod(). There are even objects called Expandos that are wholly created at runtime. Enjoy Groovy-style metaprogramming at its finest.

10.1 Discovering the Class

```
def s = "Hello"
println s.class
===> java.lang.String
```

Every object in Java has a getClass() method. In Groovy, you can shorten the call to class. (See Section 4.2, *Getter and Setter Shortcut Syntax*, on page 62 for more on this.)

Notice in this example that you use duck typing to declare the variable s—def instead of String. Even so, the variable correctly identifies itself as a String when asked. (For more information, see Section 3.5, *Optional Datatype Declaration (Duck Typing)*, on page 37.)

Once you have the class, you can ask it all sorts of interesting questions. For the record, all this is available to you via the boring old java.lang.Class class. Groovy just adds the each() syntactic sugar for iteration, as well as the default it variable. (For more information, see Section 3.14, *List Shortcuts*, on page 48.)

```
String.constructors.each{println it}
===>
public java.lang.String()
public java.lang.String(char[])
public java.lang.String(byte[])
public java.lang.String(java.lang.StringBuffer)
public java.lang.String(java.lang.StringBuilder)
public java.lang.String(java.lang.String)
...

String.interfaces.each{println it}
===>
interface java.io.Serializable
interface java.lang.Comparable
interface java.lang.CharSequence
```

10.2 Discovering the Fields of a Class

```
def d = new Date()
println d.properties
===> {month=8, day=6, calendarDate=2007-09-01T08:38:55.348-0600,
time=1188657535348, timeImpl=1188657535348, class=class java.util.Date,
timezoneOffset=360, date=1, hours=8, minutes=38, year=107,
julianCalendar=sun.util.calendar.JulianCalendar@d085f8, seconds=55}
```

Calling getProperties() on a class returns a java.util.HashMap of all the fields. For slightly prettier output, you can call each() on the HashMap. (Recall that it is the default iterator variable, as we discussed in Section 3.14, *Iterating*, on page 49.)

```
d.properties.each{println it}
===>
month=8
day=6
calendarDate=2007-09-01T08:38:55.348-0600
time=1188657535348
timeImpl=1188657535348
class=class java.util.Date
timezoneOffset=360
date=1
hours=8
minutes=38
year=107
julianCalendar=sun.util.calendar.JulianCalendar@d085f8
seconds=55
```

Java offers you a way to do almost the same thing. Every java.lang.Class offers a getDeclaredFields() method that returns an array of java.lang.reflect.Field objects.

```
d.class.declaredFields.each{println it}
===>
private static final sun.util.calendar.BaseCalendar java.util.Date.gcal
private static sun.util.calendar.BaseCalendar java.util.Date.jcal
private transient long java.util.Date.fastTime
private transient sun.util.calendar.BaseCalendar$Date java.util.Date.cdate
private static int java.util.Date.defaultCenturyStart
private static final long java.util.Date.serialVersionUID
private static final java.lang.String[] java.util.Date.wtb
private static final int[] java.util.Date.ttb
```

Wait a second...how come the getProperties call doesn't match the getDeclaredFields call? Perhaps the Javadocs[3] on the latter method can shed some light on the issue: "getDeclaredFields() returns an array

---

3. http://java.sun.com/javase/6/docs/api/java/lang/Class.html#getDeclaredFields()

of Field objects reflecting all the fields declared by the class or interface represented by this Class object. This includes public, protected, default (package) access, and private fields, but *excludes inherited fields*."

Although the Java method is technically more correct—the fields month, day, and year are technically part of an internal class—the Groovy method getProperties simply picks up the getters and setters on the class. Even though they aren't really fields of the Date object, the API designer seems to want you to treat the object as if it *did* have those fields. Both methods are presented here so that you can choose the method that best suits your needs.

Groovy's MetaClass Field

```
class Person{
  String firstname
  String lastname
}
def p = new Person(firstname:"John", lastname:"Smith")
p.properties.each{println it}
===>
firstname=John
lastname=Smith
class=class Person
metaClass=groovy.lang.MetaClassImpl@ebd7c4[class Person]
```

Calling getProperties() on a Java class returns exactly the number of fields you would expect. In Groovy, one more interesting field of note appears: metaClass.

You shouldn't be surprised in the least to see firstname and lastname appear in the list. You might not expect to see class in the list, but recall from the previous section that getProperties() returns all inherited fields on an object, not just the ones you define. Since Person extends java.lang.Object, you see the getClass() method appear here as if it were a field on the Person class.

It is the last unexpected field—the MetaClass—that makes Groovy special. All Groovy classes implement the groovy.lang.GroovyObject interface. It is the getMetaClass() method on this interface that is responsible for bringing your last unexpected field to the party.

MetaClass is what makes Groovy a dynamic language. It is what allows new fields and methods to be added to classes at runtime instead of compile time. It is what allows you to add methods like execute() and toURL() to a java.lang.String, even though it is a Final class.

Starting with the next section—Section 10.3, *Checking for the Existence of a Field*—and continuing through the rest of this chapter, the power of the MetaClass will slowly unfold. You'll see how to get it here. We'll discuss what you can do with it throughout the rest of the chapter.

MetaClasses for Java Classes

```
// in Groovy 1.0
GroovySystem.metaClassRegistry.getMetaClass(Date)

// in Groovy 1.5
Date.metaClass
```

Java objects in Groovy 1.0 don't expose a MetaClass easily, but they all still have one. To find it, you have to query the MetaClassRegistry for the JDK class. In Groovy 1.5, this process has been greatly simplified—you simply ask the class, Groovy or Java, directly for its MetaClass.

10.3 Checking for the Existence of a Field

```
class Person{
  String firstname
  String lastname
}
def p = new Person()
if(p.metaClass.hasProperty(p, "firstname")){
  p.firstname = "Jane"
}
println p.firstname
===> Jane

p.last = "Doe"
ERROR: groovy.lang.MissingPropertyException: No such property:
  last for class: Person
```

Every java.lang.Class has a getField() method that returns the field if it exists. If the call fails, it throws a java.lang.NoSuchFieldException. Groovy allows you to be a bit more fail-safe by querying the class before making the call. Calling the hasProperty() method on the MetaClass returns the field if it exists and returns null if it does not.

As discussed in Section 3.10, *Groovy Truth*, on page 44, a null response evaluates to false, allowing you to be both cautious *and* dynamic. This technique is exactly what JavaScript developers have done for years to ensure that their code works across different browsers.

Groovy 1.0 Workaround

```
if(p.properties.containsKey("firstname")){
  p.firstname = "Jane"
}
```

The hasProperty() method came along in Groovy 1.5. In Groovy 1.0, you can effectively do the same check using the containsKey() method on the HashMap returned by the getProperties() method.

When Would You Use This?

```
// url to test this code:
http://localhost:8080/groovlets/person.groovy?
    firstname=Scott&lastname=Davis&title=Bench+Warmer

// person.groovy
class Person{
  String firstname
  String lastname
  String toString(){"${firstname} ${lastname}"}
}

def person = new Person()

request.parameterMap.each{name, value->
  if(person.metaClass.hasProperty(person, name)){
    person.setProperty(name, value[0])
  }
}

println "QueryString: ${request.queryString}"
println "<br/>"
println "Incoming parameters: ${request.parameterMap}"
println "<br/>"
println "Resulting Person: ${person}"
```

Dynamically determining which fields a class has helps tremendously when you are populating it on the fly. For example, here is a simple Groovlet that fills in a class based on name/value pairs passed in via the query string. (In Figure 10.1, on the facing page, you can see the rendered results in a browser.)

This is a problem that every web framework in existence has to solve. But even if you're not doing web development, this technique is equally handy. Anytime you dynamically populate a POGO—be it from XML, CSV, a hashmap, or anything else—you should politely ask the POGO whether it can handle the data stream rather than brusquely ramming it down its throat.

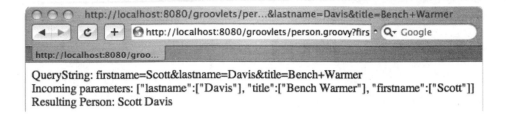

QueryString: firstname=Scott&lastname=Davis&title=Bench+Warmer
Incoming parameters: ["lastname":["Davis"], "title":["Bench Warmer"], "firstname":["Scott"]]
Resulting Person: Scott Davis

Figure 10.1: A GROOVLET DEMONSTRATING THE VALUE OF HASPROPERTY()

To begin, you define the Person class and instantiate it. Next, you walk
through the QueryString value by value. Based on the URL in the example, you should find firstname, lastname, and title entries in the query
string. If you simply walked the key list and blithely called setProperty()
on the person, bad things would happen by the time you reached title
since person doesn't have a title field. (Specifically, Groovy would complain with a groovy.lang.MissingPropertyException.) Wrapping the setProp-
erty() call in a hasProperty() check ensures that only the fields that person
knows how to deal with are injected. All unmatched fields are simply
discarded.

If you want to make the code a wee bit prettier, you can add a hasProp-
erty() convenience method right on the person class:

```
// person.groovy
class Person{
  String firstname
  String lastname
  String toString(){"${firstname} ${lastname}"}

  MetaProperty hasProperty(String property){
    return this.metaClass.hasProperty(this, property)
  }
}

def person = new Person()

request.parameterMap.each{name, value->
  if(person.hasProperty(name)){
    person.setProperty(name, value[0])
  }
}

println "QueryString: ${request.queryString}"
println "<br/>"
println "Incoming parameters: ${request.parameterMap}"
println "<br/>"
println "Resulting Person: ${person}"
```

For more information on Groovlets, see Section 2.6, *Running Groovy on a Web Server (Groovlets)*, on page 22. For more on query strings, see Section 9.4, *Working with Query Strings*, on page 150.

10.4 Discovering the Methods of a Class

```
def d = new Date()
d.class.methods.each{println it}
===>
...
public void java.util.Date.setTime(long)
public long java.util.Date.getTime()
public int java.util.Date.getYear()
public int java.util.Date.getMonth()
public int java.util.Date.getDate()
public int java.util.Date.getHours()
public int java.util.Date.getMinutes()
public int java.util.Date.getSeconds()
...
```

Every Class has a getMethods() method. Iterating through this list is no different from iterating through the fields like we discussed in Section 10.2, *Discovering the Fields of a Class*, on page 175.

You can simplify your list a bit if you just show the method names:

```
d.class.methods.name
===>
[hashCode, compareTo, compareTo, equals, toString, clone, parse,
after, before, setTime, getTime, getYear, getMonth, getDate, getHours,
getMinutes, getSeconds, UTC, setYear, setMonth, setDate, getDay, setHours,
setMinutes, setSeconds, toLocaleString, toGMTString, getTimezoneOffset,
getClass, wait, wait, wait, notify, notifyAll]
```

Dynamically Calling Methods on a Class Using Evaluate

```
def d = new Date()
d.class.methods.each{method ->
  if(method.name.startsWith("get")){
    print "${method.name}: "
    evaluate("dd = new Date(); println dd.${method.name}()")
  }
}
===>
getTime: 1188665901916
getYear: 107
getMonth: 8
getDate: 1
getHours: 10
getMinutes: 58
```

```
getSeconds: 21
getDay: 6
getTimezoneOffset: 360
getClass: class java.util.Date
```

In Section 5.10, *Evaluating a String*, on page 86, we talked about running Groovy code by evaluating an arbitrary String. What if you want to walk through all the methods on your Date object and dynamically execute all the getters? This example does the trick.

Although this code works as expected, did you notice the fast one I pulled on you in the evaluate statement? You have multiple Date instances in play here: the d instance whose methods you iterate through and a separate dd that gets instantiated each time in the loop. You had to do this because each evaluate creates its own groovy.lang. GroovyShell, and unfortunately it can't see the d variable. If you try to call d.${method.name}(), you'll get an error message:

```
Caught: groovy.lang.MissingPropertyException:
No such property: d for class: Script1
```

Script1 is the anonymous script created by the evaluate call.

There's a second way to solve this issue—one that reuses the same Date instance. In the sidebar on page 19, we talked about the groovy.lang. Binding class. This is essentially a hashmap of values that you can pass into the constructor of a GroovyShell. With just a few more lines of code, you can ensure that d is visible to the evaluate method call:

```
def d = new Date()
def binding = new Binding()
binding.setVariable("d", d)
def gs = new GroovyShell(binding)

d.class.methods.each{method ->
  if(method.name.startsWith("get")){
    print "${method.name}: "
    gs.evaluate("println d.${method.name}()")
  }
}
```

Dynamically Calling Methods on a Class Using a GString

```
def d = new Date()
d.class.methods.each{method ->
  if(method.name.startsWith("get")){
    print "${method.name}: "
    println d."${method.name}"()
  }
}
```

It's important to understand the subtle points around evaluate, Groovy-Shell, and Binding, but it's also important never to forget the power of the GString. This is the easiest, most concise way to dynamically call a method on a class—put it into a GString, and let the runtime evaluation of the statement do the rest.

Additional Methods of a Groovy Class

```
class Person{
  String firstname
  String lastname
}
def p = new Person()
p.class.methods.name
===> [getMetaClass, setMetaClass, invokeMethod, getFirstname,
setFirstname, getLastname, setLastname, setProperty, getProperty,
hashCode, getClass, equals, toString, wait, wait, wait, notify, notifyAll]
```

Let's evaluate this list of methods found on a Groovy object. The getters and setters for the fields are no surprise:

```
getFirstname, setFirstname, getLastname, setLastname
```

The methods from java.lang.Object and java.lang.Class are present and accounted for:

```
hashCode, getClass, equals, toString, wait, wait, wait, notify, notifyAll
```

What is left are the additions from groovy.lang.GroovyObject:

```
getMetaClass, setMetaClass, invokeMethod, setProperty, getProperty
```

10.5 Checking for the Existence of a Method

```
class Person{
  String firstname
  String lastname
}
def p = new Person()
if(p.metaClass.respondsTo(p, "getFirstname")){
  println p.getFirstname()
}

p.foo()
ERROR: groovy.lang.MissingMethodException: No signature of method:
  Person.foo() is applicable for argument types: () values: {}
```

As we did in Section 10.3, *Checking for the Existence of a Field*, on page 177, you can use the MetaClass to dynamically verify the existence of a method before you call it by using the respondsTo method. This method was added in Groovy 1.5.

Groovy 1.0

```
def list = p.class.methods as List
if(list.contains("getFirstname")){
  p.getFirstname()
}
```

For Groovy 1.0 users, you can accomplish the same thing by querying the list of methods on the class. Since getMethods() technically returns an array, you return it as a list so that you can use the convenient contains() method.

When Would You Use This?

We discussed duck typing in Section 3.5, *Optional Datatype Declaration (Duck Typing)*, on page 37. Java is a statically typed language, which means that all the behavior of a class is defined at compile time. Groovy is a dynamically typed language, which means that behavior can be added at runtime that didn't exist when the classes were compiled. (See Section 10.8, *Calling Methods That Don't Exist (invokeMethod)*, on page 185 for an example of this.) In simple terms, this means it is not necessary for you to *be* a duck (Duck d = new Duck()) as long as you *walk* and *quack* like a duck (respondsTo("walk") && respondsTo("quack")) at runtime.

Checking for Overloaded Methods

```
class Greeting{
  def sayHello(){
    println "Hello, Stranger"
  }

  def sayHello(String name){
    println "Hello, ${name}"
  }
}

def g = new Greeting()
if(g.metaClass.respondsTo(g, "sayHello", null)){
  g.sayHello()
}
===> Hello, Stranger

if(g.metaClass.respondsTo(g, "sayHello", String)){
  g.sayHello("Jane")
}
===> Hello, Jane
```

```
println "Number of sayHello() methods: " +
  g.metaClass.respondsTo(g, "sayHello").size()
===> Number of sayHello() methods: 2

g.metaClass.respondsTo(g, "sayHello").each{m ->
  println "${m.name} ${m.nativeParameterTypes}"
}
===>
sayHello {class java.lang.String}
sayHello {}
```

If your class has several overloaded methods, you can pass additional parameters to the respondsTo method—one for each parameter's unique datatype. If the method doesn't accept any parameters (such as say-Hello()), you pass in null for the parameter check.

If you want to see whether Greeting has a sayHello(String name1, String name2) method before you call it, try this:

```
if(g.metaClass.respondsTo(g, "sayHello", String, String)){
  g.sayHello("Jane", "Doe")
}
```

This technique is exactly what JavaScript developers have done for years to ensure that their code works across different browsers.

10.6 Creating a Field Pointer

```
class Person{
  String name
  String getName(){
    "My name is ${name}"
  }
}

def p = new Person()
p.name = "Jane"
println p.name
===> My name is Jane
println p.@name
===> Jane
```

When you write p.name, you are calling p.getName(). If you want to bypass encapsulation and access the field directly (even if it is private!), simply prefix the name of the field with an @. For example: p.@name.

You should exercise great caution in using this—breaking encapsulation is nothing that should be done on a whim. It can yield unpredictable results if the getter or setter is doing anything other than directly setting the value of the attribute.

10.7 Creating a Method Pointer

```
def list = []
def insert = list.&add
insert "Java"
insert "Groovy"
println list
===> ["Java", "Groovy"]
```

Groovy allows you to create a pointer to a method by using an & prefix. In this example, insert is an alias for list.&add(). This allows you to create your own domain-specific language. The fact that Groovy allows optional parentheses (see Section 3.3, *Optional Parentheses*, on page 34) and optional semicolons (see Section 3.2, *Optional Semicolons*, on page 32) makes this seem less like a programming language and more like plain English.

One of my favorite features of Groovy—println "Hello"—wouldn't exist if Groovy couldn't alias calls to System.out.println().

For more on DSLs, see the sidebar on page 33.

10.8 Calling Methods That Don't Exist (invokeMethod)

```
class Person{
  String name
  Map relationships = [:]

  Object invokeMethod(String what, Object who){
    if(relationships.containsKey(what)){
      who.each{thisPerson ->
        relationships.get(what).add(thisPerson)
      }
    }
    else{
      relationships.put(what,who as List)
    }
  }
}
```

```
def scott = new Person(name:"Scott")
scott.married "Kim"
scott.knows "Neal"
scott.workedWith "Brian"
scott.knows "Venkat"
scott.workedWith "Jared"
scott.knows "Ted", "Ben", "David"

println scott.relationships
===>
["married":["Kim"],
 "knows":["Neal", "Venkat", "Ted", "Ben", "David"],
 "workedWith":["Brian", "Jared"]]
```

With invokeMethod(), you can begin to see the power of dynamic languages. In this example, you want complete flexibility in how you define relationships with Person. If you want to say scott.likesToEatSushiWith "Chris", you don't want to have to create a likesToEatSushiWith() method and statically compile it into the class. You want to be able to create new types of relationships on the fly.

While the relationshipsMap gives you the flexibility to store arbitrary name/value pairs, having to write scott.put("onceWentRollerSkatingWith", "Megan") isn't as elegant as scott.onceWentRollerSkatingWith "Megan".

invokeMethod(String name, Object args) is at the heart of Groovy metaprogramming. Every method call on an object is intercepted by invoke-Method. The name parameter is the method call (married, knows, and workedWith). The args parameter is an Object array that catches all subsequent parameters (Kim, Neal, and Brian).

Without invokeMethod(), none of the parsers or slurpers discussed in Chapter 7, *Parsing XML*, on page 107 would work as elegantly as they do, allowing you to call the child XML elements as if they were method calls on the parent node.

10.9 Creating an Expando

```
def e = new Expando()
e.class
===> class groovy.util.Expando
e.properties
===> {}
e.class.methods.name
===> [invokeMethod, getMetaPropertyValues, hashCode, equals,
toString, setProperty, getProperty, getProperties, getMetaClass,
setMetaClass, getClass, wait, wait, wait, notify, notifyAll]
```

Expandos are curious little creatures. They are blank slates—objects that are just waiting for you to attach new fields and methods to them. You can see that after you create them, they have no fields to speak of and only the basic methods that they inherit from java.lang.Object and groovy.lang.GroovyObject.

So then, what are they good for?

```
e.latitude = 70
e.longitude = 30
println e
===> {longitude=30, latitude=70}
```

Expandos will magically *expand* to support any fields you need. You simply attach the field to the object, and your expando begins to take shape. (Dynamic languages such as JavaScript use this to great effect.)

And what about methods? Simply add a new closure to the expando. (See Section 3.17, *Closures and Blocks*, on page 57 for more information.)

```
e.areWeLost = {->
  return (e.longitude != 30) || (e.latitude != 70)
}

e.areWeLost()
===> false

e.latitude = 12
e.areWeLost()
===> true
```

In this example, the areWeLost closure accepts no arguments. Here is an example of a closure that takes a single parameter:

```
e.goNorth = { howMuch ->
  e.latitude += howMuch
}

println e.latitude
===> 12

e.goNorth(20)
===> 32
```

10.10 Adding Methods to a Class Dynamically (Categories)

```
use(RandomHelper){
  15.times{ println 10.rand() }
}

class RandomHelper{
  static int rand(Integer self){
    def r = new Random()
    return r.nextInt(self.intValue())
  }
}
===> 5 2 7 0 7 8 2 3 5 1 7 8 9 8 1
```

Categories allow you to add new functionality to any class at runtime. This means you can add those *missing* methods that the original author *forgot*—even if you don't have access to the original source code.

In this example, we add a rand() method to the Integer class. Calling 10.rand() returns a random number from 0 to 9. Calling 100.rand() does the same from 0 to 99. You get the idea. Any Integer inside the use block gets this method automatically. Anything outside the use block is unaffected.

Notice that there is nothing special about the RandomHelper class—it doesn't extend any magical parent class or implement a special interface. The only requirement is that the methods all must accept an instance of themselves (self) as the first argument. This type of class is called a *category* in Groovy.

Using pure Java, you'd be blocked from adding new behavior directly to the java.lang.Integer class for a couple of reasons. First, your chances of adding the rand() method to the source code of Integer, compiling it, and getting widespread distribution is pretty slim. ("Hey, which version of Java does your application require?" "Uh, 1.5. Scott...how many servers do you have with that version in production?")

OK, so modifying the source code is ruled out. The next logical step is to extend Integer, right? Well, it would be if Integer weren't declared final. (D'oh!) So, using a pure Java solution, you are left to create your own com.mycompany.Integer class that wraps a java.lang.Integer with your custom behavior. The problem with this solution is that because of Java's strong typing, you cannot polymorphically swap Sun's Integer out for your own. This six-line solution is looking better all the time, isn't it?

A Slightly More Advanced Category Example

```
use(InternetUtils){
  println "http://localhost:8080/".get()
  println "http://search.yahoo.com/search".get("p=groovy")

  def params = [:]
  params.n = "10"
  params.vl = "lang_eng"
  params.p = "groovy"
  println "http://search.yahoo.com/search".get(params)
}

class InternetUtils{
  static String get(String self){
    return self.toURL().text
  }

  static String get(String self, String queryString){
    def url = self + "?" + queryString
    return url.get()
  }

  static String get(String self, Map params){
    def list = []
    params.each{k,v->
      list << "$k=" + URLEncoder.encode(v)
    }
    def url = self + "?" + list.join("&")
    return url.get()
  }
}
```

In this example, you define an InternetUtils class that offers a couple of new methods: a no-argument get method that converts any String to a URL object and performs an HTTP GET request, an overloaded get method that accepts a String as a query string, and finally an overloaded get method that constructs a well-formed query string out of the params hashmap. (For more on using Groovy to streamline HTTP GET requests, see Section 9.3, *Making an HTTP GET Request*, on page 146.)

The use block keeps the new functionality narrowly scoped. You don't have to worry about your new methods sneaking out to all Strings across your entire application. >Of course, if you *do* want to globally apply these new methods to all Strings, see Section 10.11, *Adding Methods to a Class Dynamically (ExpandoMetaClass)*, on the next page.

You can use as many categories as you want in a single use block. Simply pass a comma-separated list to the use block:

```
use(RandomHelper, InternetUtils, SomeOtherCategory) { ... }
```

Categories are just as *useful* in Java as they are in Groovy. (Sorry, I couldn't resist the pun.) InternetUtils is a pretty handy class to have around in either language. There is nothing that explicitly ties it to Groovy. The use block, of course, is pure Groovy syntactic sugar, but the Category class can be used anywhere you need it in either language.

Mixing in new functionality to any class is now at your fingertips. Once you get hooked on this new programming paradigm, you'll wonder how you ever lived without it. (See Section 8.14, *Parsing Complex CSV*, on page 140 for another example of categories in action.)

10.11 Adding Methods to a Class Dynamically (ExpandoMetaClass)

```
Integer.metaClass.rand = {->
  def r = new Random()
  return r.nextInt(delegate.intValue())
}

15.times{ println 10.rand() }
===> 2 5 5 5 8 7 2 9 1 4 0 9 9 0 8
```

In Section 10.2, *Groovy's MetaClass Field*, on page 176, we learned that every class in Groovy has a MetaClass. In Section 10.9, *Creating an Expando*, on page 186, we learned about malleable objects that can have new methods added to them on the fly. The ExpandoMetaClass class combines these two concepts—every class's MetaClass can be extended at runtime like an expando. In this example, we add the rand() method directly to Integer's MetaClass. This means that all Integers in the running application now have a rand() method.

When using categories (as discussed in Section 10.10, *Adding Methods to a Class Dynamically (Categories)*, on page 188), each method must have a self parameter. When using ExpandoMetaClass, the delegate serves this role. The this keyword gives you the MetaClass—delegate gives you one class up in the chain. In this particular case, the call to delegate gives you 10.

A Slightly More Advanced ExpandoMetaClass Example

```
String.metaClass.get = {->
  return delegate.toURL().text
}

String.metaClass.get = {String queryString ->
  def url = delegate + "?" + queryString
  return url.get()
}

String.metaClass.get = {Map params ->
  def list = []
  params.each{k,v->
    list << "$k=" + URLEncoder.encode(v)
  }
  def url = delegate + "?" + list.join("&")
  return url.get()
}


println "http://localhost:8080/".get()
println "http://search.yahoo.com/search".get("p=groovy")

def params = [:]
params.n = "10"
params.vl = "lang_eng"
params.p = "groovy"
println "http://search.yahoo.com/search".get(params)
```

In terms of functionality, the three methods here are identical to the examples found in Section 10.10, *Adding Methods to a Class Dynamically (Categories)*, on page 188. In terms of implementation, you're faced with code that is firmly grounded in Groovy syntax and idioms. The self references have all been changed to delegate. Closures are used as opposed to static methods grouped together in a category class.

So, which should you use—a category or ExpandoMetaClass? The answer is "It depends." (Isn't that *always* the answer?) A category is perfect if you want to limit the scope of your new methods to a well-defined block of code. An ExpandoMetaClass is better if you want to have your new methods applied to all instances across the entire running application. If you want your new functionality to be easily shared by both Java and Groovy code, categories leave you with a plain old Java class with static methods. ExpandoMetaClasses are more closely tied to Groovy, but they are significantly more performant as well.

Chapter 11

Working with Grails

Up to this point, we've been focusing on Groovy. In this chapter, we introduce Grails. All of the lessons we learned about the core language will now be applied to this modern web framework.

The Grails story is similar to the Groovy story—you get seamless integration with Java classes, you use standard JEE technologies such as WAR files, you deploy to standard servlet containers, and so on.

Grails is based on popular libraries such as Spring and Hibernate, so you don't have to check your experience with these APIs at the door. But just as Groovy has a few new tricks up its sleeve, Grails does as well. It uses *convention over configuration*[1] to virtually eliminate XML files such as struts-config.xml. It offers a new twist on Ant builds in GANT—a pure Groovy implementation of Ant. It wraps Hibernate in a Groovy API it calls GORM—the Grails Object/Relational Mapper.

What Groovy does for Java development, Grails does for web development. You'll be amazed at how quickly you can have a new web application up and running. Let's dive right in!

---

1. http://en.wikipedia.org/wiki/Convention_over_Configuration

11.1 Installing Grails

1. Download and unzip grails.zip from http://grails.org.
2. Create a GRAILS_HOME environment variable.
3. Add $GRAILS_HOME/bin to the PATH.

Does this sound vaguely familiar? It should—these are the same steps you take to install Groovy; only the names have changed. (See Section 2.1, *Installing Groovy*, on page 13 for details.) Everything you need to install Grails is included in the single ZIP file.

Interestingly, you don't even need to have Groovy installed separately on your system to run Grails. As discussed in Section 4.8, *Calling Groovy from Java*, on page 69, the way to Groovy-enable a Java project is to drop the single Groovy JAR from $GROOVY_HOME/embeddable into your CLASSPATH. In this case, the Groovy JAR included in the Grails ZIP file ends up in WEB-INF/lib alongside spring.jar, hibernate.jar, and the rest of the dependencies. You don't have to do a thing to Groovy-enable Grails—it is Groovy-enabled out of the box.

You will, however, need to have a JDK installed. Grails 1.*x* runs on all modern versions of Java—1.4, 1.5, and 1.6. If you are running an older version of Java, visit http://java.sun.com for an update. If you don't know which version of Java you have installed, type java -version at a command prompt:

```
$ java -version
===>
java version "1.5.0_13"
Java(TM) 2 Runtime Environment, Standard Edition (build 1.5.0_13-b05-237)
Java HotSpot(TM) Client VM (build 1.5.0_13-119, mixed mode, sharing)
```

To take advantage of Java 1.5 language features, you'll need at least a 1.5 JDK under the covers. Grails runs noticeably faster on each new generation of the JVM. I strongly recommend running Grails on the most recent version of Java that you can.

To install Grails on your operating system, see Section 11.1, *Installing Grails on Unix, Linux, and Mac OS X*, on page 196 or Section 11.1, *Installing Grails on Windows*, on page 197.

Checking the Grails Version

```
$ grails -version

Welcome to Grails 1.0 - http://grails.org/
Licensed under Apache Standard License 2.0
Grails home is set to: /opt/grails
```

```
Base Directory: /svn/src
/svn/src does not appear to be part of a Grails application.
The following commands are supported outside of a project:
        create-app
        create-plugin
        help
        list-plugins
        package-plugin
        plugin-info
        set-proxy
Run 'grails help' for a complete list of available scripts.
```

To check the version of Grails you are running, type grails -version. Notice that the grails command recognizes that it isn't being run from the root directory of a Grails project. In Section 11.2, *Creating Your First Grails App*, on page 197, we'll explore the grails create-app command in greater detail. In Section 12.6, *Installing Plug-Ins*, on page 241, we'll explore Grails plug-ins. grails help, as you might imagine, gives you a full list of all available Grails commands:

```
$ grails help
...
Usage (optionals marked with *):
grails [environment]* [target] [arguments]*

Examples:
grails dev run-app
grails create-app books

Available Targets (type grails help 'target-name' for more info):
grails bootstrap
grails bug-report
grails clean
grails compile
grails console
grails create-app
grails create-controller
grails create-domain-class
grails create-integration-test
grails create-plugin
grails create-script
grails create-service
grails create-tag-lib
grails create-unit-test
grails doc
grails generate-all
grails generate-controller
grails generate-views
grails help
grails init
```

```
grails install-plugin
grails install-templates
grails list-plugins
grails package
grails package-plugin
grails package-plugins
grails plugin-info
grails release-plugin
grails run-app
grails run-app-https
grails set-proxy
grails set-version
grails shell
grails stats
grails test-app
grails upgrade
grails war
```

Installing Grails on Unix, Linux, and Mac OS X

Download the latest Grails ZIP file (or tarball) from http://grails.org. Unzip it to the directory of your choice. I prefer /opt. You will end up with a grails directory that has the version number on the end of it, such as grails-1.0. I like creating a symlink that doesn't include the specific version number: ln -s grails-1.0 grails. This allows me to switch between versions of Grails cleanly and easily.

Since ZIP files don't preserve Unix file permissions, be sure to swing by the bin directory and make the files executable:

```
$ chmod a+x *
```

Once the directory is in place, you next need to create a GRAILS_HOME environment variable. The steps to do this vary from shell to shell. For Bash, edit either .bash_profile or .bash_rc in your home directory. Add the following:

```
### Grails
GRAILS_HOME=/opt/grails
PATH=$PATH:$GRAILS_HOME/bin
export GRAILS_HOME PATH
```

For these changes to take effect, you need to restart your terminal session. Alternately, you can type source .bash_profile to load the changes into the current session. Type echo $GRAILS_HOME to confirm that your changes took effect.

```
$ echo $GRAILS_HOME
/opt/grails
```

To verify that the Grails command is in the path, type grails -version. If you see a message similar to the one in Section 11.1, *Checking the Grails Version*, on page 194, you have successfully installed Grails.

Installing Grails on Windows

Download the latest Grails ZIP file from http://grails.org. Unzip it to the directory of your choice. I prefer c:\opt. You will end up with a grails directory that has the version number on the end of it, such as grails-1.0. Although you can rename it to something simpler like grails, I've found that keeping the version number on the directory name helps make future upgrades less ambiguous.

Once the directory is in place, you next need to create a GRAILS_HOME environment variable. For Windows XP, go to the Control Panel, and double-click System. Click the Advanced tab and then Environment Variables at the bottom of the window. In the new window, click New under System Variables. Use GRAILS_HOME for the variable name and c:\opt\grails-1.0 for the variable value.

To add Grails to the path, find the PATH variable, and double-click it. Add ;%GRAILS_HOME%\bin to the end of the variable. (Don't forget the leading semicolon.) Click OK to back out of all the dialog boxes.

For these changes to take effect, you need to exit or restart any command prompts you have open. Open a new command prompt, and type set to display a list of all environment variables. Make sure GRAILS_HOME appears.

To verify that the Grails command is in the path, type grails -version. If you see a message similar to the one in Section 11.1, *Checking the Grails Version*, on page 194, you have successfully installed Grails.

11.2 Creating Your First Grails App

```
1. $ grails create-app bookstore
2. $ cd bookstore
3. $ grails create-domain-class book
4. add fields to bookstore/grails-app/domain/Book.groovy
5. $ grails generate-all Book
6. $ grails run-app
```

You'll be amazed at how quickly you can have your first Grails application up and running—60 seconds or less is no exaggeration.

Step 1: Creating the Initial Application

```
$ grails create-app bookstore
```

Make sure you are in a clean directory, and then type grails create-app bookstore. This, of course, assumes you want your application to be named bookstore. The name you supply will be used for the URL, the WAR file that gets generated, and all manner of other things. It can be easily overridden in the bookstore/application.properties file that gets generated along with the rest of the standard directory structure, but as you can see, convention over configuration comes into play before you even write a single line of code.

```
// application.properties
app.version=0.1
app.servlet.version=2.4
app.grails.version=1.0
app.name=bookstore
```

Step 2: Exploring the Directory Structure

```
$ cd bookstore
$ ls -al
total 32
-rw-r--r--    application.properties
-rw-r--r--    bookstore.launch
-rw-r--r--    bookstore.tmproj
-rw-r--r--    build.xml
drwxr-xr-x    grails-app
drwxr-xr-x    lib
drwxr-xr-x    scripts
drwxr-xr-x    src
drwxr-xr-x    test
drwxr-xr-x    web-app
```

Like Maven, Rails, or AppFuse, Grails scaffolds out a standard directory structure for you. If you feel hopelessly constrained by this limitation and cannot work with a framework unless you can meticulously design your own custom directory tree, you aren't going to have much fun working with Grails.

One of the main benefits of convention over configuration is, uh, the convention part. You can sit down with any Grails application and know immediately which bits are stored in what bucket.

Directory	What It Holds
grails-app	*Models, views, controllers—all of the interesting bits of the application*
lib	*Custom JARs such as database drivers (WEB-INF/lib)*
scripts	*Custom Groovy scripts*
src	*Java source files to be compiled (WEB-INF/classes)*
test	*Unit and integration tests*
web-app	*GSPs, CSS, JavaScript, and other traditional web files*

Step 3: Creating a Domain Class

```
$ grails create-domain-class book
```

Make sure you are in the bookstore directory, and then type grails create-domain-class book. The majority of the Grails commands are context sensitive—in other words, they must be run from the root of the Grails application directory.

The result of the create-domain-class command is two stubbed out empty files: Book.groovy in bookstore/grails-app/domain and BookTests.groovy in bookstore/test/integration.

```
// Book.groovy
class Book {

}

// BookTests.groovy
class BookTests extends GroovyTestCase {
  void testSomething() {

  }
}
```

Book.groovy is where we'll focus our energies for the rest of this chapter. Testing, although important, is a topic for another book. BookTests.groovy is a GroovyTestCase, which is simply a thin Groovy facade over a JUnit 3.*x* TestCase. This means it will snap in seamlessly with your existing JUnit testing infrastructure. For more on GroovyTestCases, see the online Groovy Testing Guide.[2] For more on testing Grails applications, see the testing section in the online Grails documentation.[3]

---

2. http://groovy.codehaus.org/Testing+Guide
3. http://grails.org/doc/1.0.x/guide/single.html#9.\%20Testing

Figure 11.1: BOOK, BOOKCONTROLLER, AND BOOK VIEWS

The grails-app/domain directory is special. Every file in this directory gets persisted to a database automatically. Grails walks this directory on start-up and creates a table in the embedded HSQLDB database for each POGO it finds.

Step 4: Adding Fields to the Domain Class

```
// bookstore/grails-app/domain/Book.groovy
class Book {
  String title
  String author
  Integer pages

  String toString(){
    return "${title} by ${author}"
  }
}
```

You probably recognize this POGO from Chapter 4, *Java and Groovy Integration*, on page 59. The domain classes in a Grails app are Groovy-Beans, plain and simple. Of course, if you already have legacy JavaBeans created, you can put them in bookstore/src/java.

The interesting thing about domain classes in Grails is that they get more than just automatic getters and setters. They get instance methods such as book.save() and book.delete() that do exactly what you'd expect them to do—save and delete the corresponding record in the table. The domain classes also get static methods such as Book.get() and Book.list(). These, again, do the sort of thing they sound like they'd do. They allow you to pull a single Book out of the table or a list.

The domain classes get additional fields such as id and version to store the primary key and help with optimistic locking. You can even call methods that don't exist like Book.findByAuthor("Scott Davis") and Book.findAllByPagesBetween(500, 1000). (That sounds a lot like Section 10.8, *Calling Methods That Don't Exist (invokeMethod)*, on page 185, doesn't it?) Notice, however, that you don't have to extend a parent class or implement a magic interface. All this behavior comes about because of the wonders of metaprogramming (Chapter 10, *Metaprogramming*, on page 173).

Step 5: Generating the Controller and Views

```
$ grails generate-all Book
```

Once your domain class has all the fields it needs, you can type grails generate-all Book. This instructs Grails to create a controller and a set of views for the Book class. At this point you have all the pieces of a classic Model-View-Controller pattern.[4]

The Book.groovy domain class is the model. It holds the data in a way that is independent of any particular presentation format. The views are Groovy Server Pages (GSPs) named create.gsp, edit.gsp, list.gsp, and save.gsp. (We'll see in Section 12.1, *Returning XML*, on page 227 and Section 12.4, *Setting Up an Atom Feed*, on page 233 how you can provide many different views for the same model.) And finally, BookController.groovy does what controllers do—it makes sure the model gets the data it needs and hands it off to the appropriate view.

---

4. http://en.wikipedia.org/wiki/Model_view_controller

It helps seeing everything in context. In Figure 11.1, on page 200, you can see Book.groovy, BookController.groovy, and each of the GSPs in the views directory. There is not a single line of XML that needs to be written in order to get these classes to work together. Convention over configuration dictates that a Book model has a corresponding BookController and a corresponding set of views in the views/book directory.

As you dig deeper into these files, you'll see more autowiring in action. For instance, the list method in BookController corresponds to the list.gsp file. You still may end up using an XML configuration file on occasion (such as grails-app/conf/spring/resources.xml), but the days of baby-sitting a struts-config.xml file are a thing of the past in Grails.

Generating actual files for the controller and views is nice because you can see all the moving parts and how they interrelate. The problem with these files, however, is that they can get stale. Once you add new fields to the POGO, you have to regenerate the controller and views, or they won't match up with the model. In Section 11.8, *Understanding Controllers and Views*, on page 212, you'll see how you can dynamically scaffold out the controllers and views at runtime, in memory. This keeps everything in sync. In production, I end up using a healthy combination of files on disk and dynamically scaffolded views.

Step 6: Running the Application

```
$ grails run-app
```

OK, let's see the fruits of our labors. Type grails run-app to launch the embedded version of Jetty, your web server and servlet container. (To launch your Grails app in another container, see Section 11.5, *Generating a WAR*, on page 207.) After Jetty starts, Grails scans the grails-app/domain directory, creating new tables in the in-memory HSQLDB database. (To store things in another database, have a look at Section 11.6, *Changing Databases*, on page 208.) After a flurry of Log4j messages fly past on the console, you should be rewarded with a message that says this:

```
Server running. Browse to http://localhost:8080/bookstore
```

If you already have a server running on port 8080, you'll be scolded with a core dump that ends with this:

```
Server failed to start: java.net.BindException: Address already in use
```

Don't worry. Take a look at Section 11.4, *Running Grails on a Different Port*, on page 206 to get Jetty running somewhere else.

Figure 11.2: THE GRAILS WELCOME SCREEN

Anytime you want to shut down the server, simply press Ctrl+C.

Once you have the application up and running, visit http://localhost:8080/bookstore in a web browser. You'll be greeted by the stock welcome screen. (See Figure 11.2.) Every subsequent controller you create will be automatically added to this page. Open bookstore/web-app/index.gsp, and you'll see a familiar each iteration going on with an interesting twist: GSPs have a <g:each> tag that is the equivalent of the List.each closure discussed in Section 3.14, *List Shortcuts*, on page 48. Each item (<li>) in the bulleted/unordered list (<ul>) is a controller from the grailsApplication.getControllerClasses() call.

```
<ul>
  <g:each var="c" in="${grailsApplication.controllerClasses}">
    <li class="controller">
      <g:link controller="${c.logicalPropertyName}">${c.fullName}</g:link>
    </li>
  </g:each>
</ul>
```

We'll see how to change the default home page in Section 11.7, *Changing the Home Page*, on page 211.

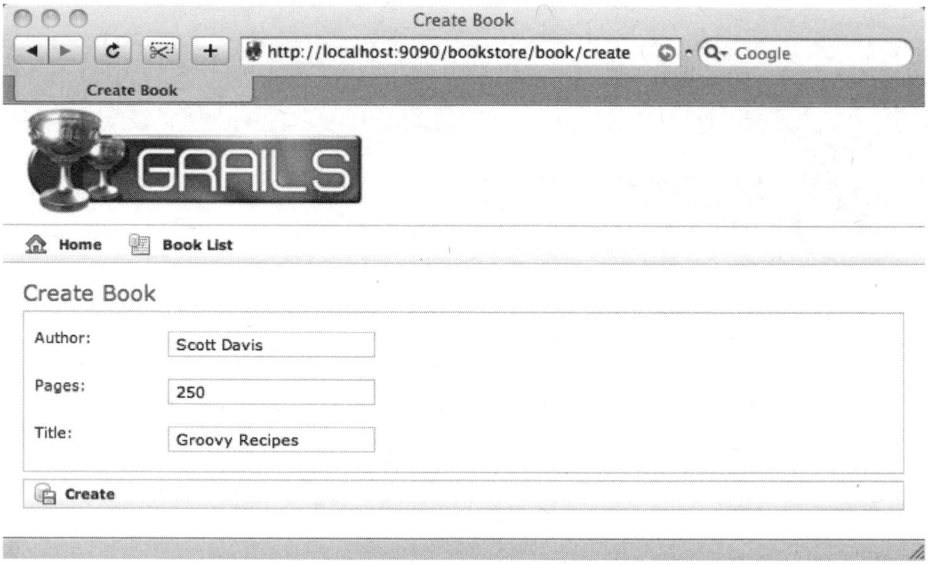

Figure 11.3: CREATING A NEW BOOK

Click the BookController link, and you'll be presented with an empty list of Books. Let's fix that problem. Click New Book, and fill in the blanks. (See Figure 11.3.) This, of course, is grails-app/views/create.gsp. We'll look more at GSPs in Section 11.8, *Understanding Controllers and Views*, on page 212.

Clicking Create brings you to the show page—grails-app/views/show.gsp. From here you can either create a new book or head back to the list page. (See Figure 11.4, on the facing page.) You probably also noticed that you can edit or delete the book as well.

So, you get a full CRUD application in less than 60 seconds. More important, you get a full CRUD application in, what, less than a dozen lines of typing? And this application uses Spring and Hibernate, both well-understood Java libraries. This application is a standard WAR file, able to be deployed on any standard servlet container or application server (Tomcat, Jetty, JBoss, Geronimo, WebSphere, WebLogic, and so on). This application can talk to any database that has a JDBC driver and a Hibernate dialect. All Groovy does is provide a bit of glue code to hold everything together.

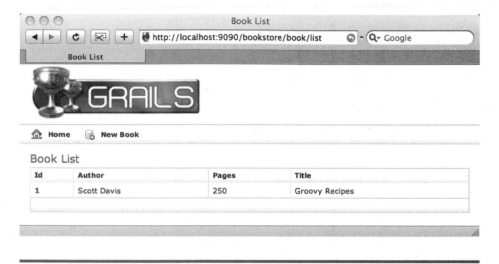

Figure 11.4: A LIST OF BOOKS

In order to get a quick snapshot of the size of your new application, type grails stats:

```
$ grails stats
+---------------------+-------+-------+
| Name                | Files | LOC   |
+---------------------+-------+-------+
| Controllers         |     1 |    66 |
| Domain Classes      |     1 |     8 |
| Integration Tests   |     1 |     4 |
+---------------------+-------+-------+
| Totals              |     3 |    78 |
+---------------------+-------+-------+
```

Overall, we have an interesting little web framework on our hands that mixes the familiar with the cutting edge. Not bad, not bad.

11.3 Understanding Grails Environments

```
$ grails run-app
$ grails dev  run-app // the default environment
$ grails test run-app
$ grails prod run-app
```

Grails ships with three standard *environments*—development, test, and production. These environments make it easy to change things such as database connections and Log4j settings based on the *mode* in which you're running. Each environment also has distinct behavior: in dev mode, all files get reloaded automatically. This means you can make changes to your code without having to bounce the server. But this dynamic reloading comes a bit of a cost in terms of performance, so prod mode is optimized for speed instead of flexibility.

To see per-environment configuration settings, look no further than grails-app/conf/DataSource.groovy. (For an example of DataSource.groovy, see Section 11.6, *Changing Databases*, on page 208.) Settings outside the environments block are global. Settings inside blocks such as development can selectively override the global settings.

Although there is no environments block in grails-app/conf/Config.groovy, you can add one yourself. Type the following at the top of the file:

```
environments{
  production{
    println "I'm in production"
  }
  foo{
    println "I'm in foo"
  }
}
```

Save the file, and then type grails prod run-app. You should see I'm in production show up early in the console output.

Custom Environments

```
$ grails -Dgrails.env=foo run-app
```

The three default environments are supported natively at the command line. If you set up a custom environment, you have just a bit more typing to do. You have to set the grails.env property yourself by using the customary -D flag. If you added the code to Config.groovy in the previous section, typing grails -Dgrails.env=foo run-app should give you I'm in foo in the console output.

11.4 Running Grails on a Different Port

```
$ grails -Dserver.port=9090 run-app
```

```
-- OR --
```

```
$GRAILS_HOME/scripts/Init.groovy
```

Grails tries to run on port 8080 by default. You can override this from the command line by explicitly passing in an alternate server.port via the -D flag. This is nice for ad hoc testing—you can run several servers on the same physical machine...one on 6060, another on 7070, and so on.

If, however, you always want to run Grails on port 9090, this extra bit of typing quickly becomes tedious and error-prone. You can set the default at the source in $GRAILS_HOME/scripts/Init.groovy.

```
serverPort = System.getProperty('server.port') ?
             System.getProperty('server.port').toInteger() : 9090
```

Did you notice that Init.groovy is a GANT file? GANT[5] is a Groovy implementation of Ant. If you like the conventions of Ant but prefer the expressiveness of a dynamic language over the rigidity of static XML, GANT is something you should look into.

11.5 Generating a WAR

```
$ grails war
```

Although running Grails in the embedded Jetty container is convenient for development, few companies run Jetty in production. (This, by the way, is a real shame. Jetty is a mature servlet container that is ranked regularly as one of the fastest on the market.)

Luckily, Grails can generate an industry-standard WAR file that can be deployed on any application server that you have in production. Simply type grails war, and after a bit of activity, you'll be presented with a file named bookstore-0.1.war. The version number, as well as the application name, comes from application.properties. You can change these values to whatever is appropriate.

```
// application.properties
app.version=0.1
app.servlet.version=2.4
app.grails.version=1.0
app.name=bookstore
```

It probably goes without saying that the WAR file runs in production mode. (For more information, see Section 11.3, *Understanding Grails Environments*, on page 205.)

----

5. http://gant.codehaus.org/

11.6 Changing Databases

1. Set up the database and user.
2. Copy the driver JAR into lib.
3. Adjust settings in grails-app/conf/DataSource.groovy.

The embedded database HSQLDB is great to get things up and running quickly, but most production Grails applications end up relying on an external database. The good news is if your database is supported by Hibernate, it is supported by Grails as well. The Grails Object/Relational Mapper (GORM) is a thin Groovy facade over Hibernate.

For demonstration purposes, we'll migrate our bookstore application to MySQL.[6]

Step 1: Setting Up the Database and User

```
$ mysql --user=root
mysql> create database bookstore_dev;
mysql> use bookstore_dev;
mysql> grant all on bookstore_dev.* to grails@localhost identified by 'server';
mysql> flush privileges;
mysql> quit

$ mysql --user=grails -p --database=bookstore_dev
```

Assuming that MySQL is already installed and running, you'll next want to log in as a user with administration privileges. create database bookstore_dev; creates the target database in MySQL. (While you're here, you might want to create database bookstore_prod; and create database bookstore_test;.)

Once the target database is created, you'll want to create a user. Even though the syntax shown here is MySQL specific, it still demonstrates various things you'll want to consider when setting up your own user account. grant all on bookstore_dev.* says, "I want this user that I'm creating to have all permissions on all items in the bookstore_dev database. I want them to be able to create, alter, and delete tables. I want them to be able to create indices, views, and all types of database artifacts." If you traditionally create more restricted users, you should take a look at Section 11.6, *Adjusting dbCreate*, on page 210 to get a better idea of what Grails expects to be able to do out of the box.

---

6. http://www.mysql.org

If you limit what Grails can do, you'll need to take responsibility for these tasks on your own.

The second half of the command—to grails@localhost identified by 'server'—says, "The username should be *grails*, the password should be *server*, and this user should be able to log in only from *localhost*." If you want to create an account that can log in from a remote server, try something like grails@192.168.1.1.

Finally, it's always helpful to sanity check your work by testing it by hand. If you're able to log in by typing mysql --user=grails -p --database=bookstore_dev, your user account was created successfully.

Step 2: Copying the Database Driver

```
$ cp ~/mysql-connector-java-3.1.13-bin.jar bookstore/lib
```

This is the easiest step of the three. Copy the JDBC driver JAR into the lib directory, and Grails will have the software it needs to connect to the database. The last step is to configure the connection settings.

Step 3: Adjusting the Configuration in DataSource.groovy

```
dataSource {
  pooled = false
  driverClassName = "com.mysql.jdbc.Driver"
  username = "grails"
  password = "server"
}
hibernate {
  cache.use_second_level_cache=true
  cache.use_query_cache=true
  cache.provider_class='org.hibernate.cache.EhCacheProvider'
}

// environment specific settings
environments {
  development {
    dataSource {
      // one of 'create', 'create-drop','update'
      dbCreate = "update"
      url = "jdbc:mysql://localhost:3306/bookstore_dev?autoreconnect=true"
    }
  }
  test {
    dataSource {
      dbCreate = "update"
      url = "jdbc:hsqldb:mem:testDb"
    }
  }
```

```
    production {
      dataSource {
        dbCreate = "update"
        url = "jdbc:hsqldb:file:prodDb;shutdown=true"
      }
    }
  }
```

To get Grails pointed to your newly created MySQL database, you need to adjust four values:

driverClassName	*com.mysql.jdbc.Driver*
username	*grails*
password	*server*
url	*jdbc:mysql://localhost:3306/bookstore_dev*

Recall that Grails supports modifying the configuration based on the *mode* in which it is running. (See Section 11.3, *Understanding Grails Environments*, on page 205.) In the earlier example, the driverClassName, username, and password settings are shared across all environments. This is clearly a problem since we left HSQLDB artifacts laying around in test and production that will not work with MySQL. You have two choices: you can move the MySQL-specific driverClassName, username, and password values into the development block and set up similar ones for test and production, or you change the url to a valid MySQL one in the other blocks.

Adjusting dbCreate

```
environments {
  development {
    dataSource {
      // one of 'create', 'create-drop','update'
      dbCreate = "update"
    }
  }
}
```

While you are in grails-app/conf/DataSource.groovy adjusting connection settings to your database, you might want to tweak the dbCreate value. This variable corresponds to the hibernate.hbm2ddl.auto setting in Hibernate. By default, Grails lets Hibernate create the tables that correspond to the classes in the grails-app/domain directory. dbCreate allows you to fine-tune the table generation behavior.

Setting	Start-Up	Shutdown
create-drop	*Creates tables*	*Drops tables*
create	*Creates or alters tables*	*Deletes only data*
update	*Creates or alters tables*	*Leaves data intact*

dbCreate is set to create by default for development; for test and production, it is set to update. I generally set dbCreate to update for development as well—it's a bummer always losing your data.

Bear in mind that since create and update alter the tables instead of creating them from scratch each time Grails starts up, they are conservative in the changes they'll make. They will happily add fields, but they won't delete fields. Similarly, they will lengthen fields, but they will not shorten them. Anything that might cause data loss is your responsibility to manage.

And don't worry—if your DBA breaks out in a cold sweat at the thought of Hibernate mucking around with some precious tables, commenting out the dbCreate variable turns this feature off completely. If you are dealing with legacy tables or tables that are shared with other applications, commenting out dbCreate should be the first thing you change in DataSource.groovy.

11.7 Changing the Home Page

```
// web-app/index.gsp
<% response.sendRedirect("book/list") %>
```

As nice as the default home page is while you're in development, you will probably want to customize it at some point. (See Figure 11.2, on page 203.) The default pages in a Grails app are named index.gsp.

Since Jetty is a standards-compliant servlet container, it also supports index.jsp. Be warned that if you have both an index.jsp and index.gsp in the same directory, the .jsp page takes precedence.

Oftentimes Grails apps simply redirect to one of the existing controllers. The previous example redirects to the list view of the book controller.

A slightly more robust way to change the home page is to add a custom mapping for the root URL (/) to grails-app/conf/UrlMappings.groovy:

```
// grails-app/conf/UrlMappings.groovy
class UrlMappings {
  static mappings = {
    "/" (controller:"book", action:"list")
  }
}
```

UrlMappings.groovy gives you fine-grained control over how your URLs get mapped to controllers in a Grails application. For more information, see the online documentation.[7]

11.8 Understanding Controllers and Views

```
// grails-app/controllers/BookController.groovy

class BookController {
  def list = {
    if(!params.max) params.max = 10
    [ bookList: Book.list( params ) ]
  }

  def show = {
    [ book : Book.get( params.id ) ]
  }

  ...
}
```

The controllers of a Grails application are the glue that binds the views to the models. Every URL you see—http://localhost:8080/bookstore/book/list—corresponds to an action in a controller—Bookstore.list. Notice that the Controller suffix is dropped from the name in Grails URLs. With few exceptions, the controller actions have a partner in the grails-app/views directory named the same thing—list.gsp. (The exceptions to this rule are discussed in Section 11.8, *Render*, on page 214.)

Understanding Grails controllers boils down to understand the three Rs: redirect, return, and render.

Redirect

```
def index = { redirect(action:list,params:params) }
```

---

7. http://grails.codehaus.org/URL+mapping

Every controller should have an index. This action is the default action of the controller, much like index.gsp, as discussed in Section 11.7, *Changing the Home Page*, on page 211.

In this example, we see that absent any other directive, the controller will redirect bookstore/book requests to the list action. Any accompanying QueryString parameters are stored in the params map and passed along to the action.

Redirects can also accept a controller argument. Hypothetically, if saving a book required that the user be logged in and have sufficient permissions, you could redirect the request to the Logon controller.

Return

```
def list = {
  if(!params.max) params.max = 10
  [ bookList: Book.list( params ) ]
}

def show = {
  [ book : Book.get( params.id ) ]
}
```

The last line of a Groovy method is an implicit return statement. (See Section 3.4, *Optional Return Statements*, on page 36 for more information.) The last line of a Grails action returns a Map of values to the corresponding GSP page of the same name.

In the case of the list action, if no one supplies a max parameter on the query string, it will return an ArrayList of ten Books from the database. You can see the bookList element used in list.gsp here:

```
<g:each in="${bookList}" status="i" var="book">
  <tr class="${(i % 2) == 0 ? 'odd' : 'even'}">
    <td>
      <g:link action="show" id="${book.id}">${book.id?.encodeAsHTML()}</g:link>
    </td>
    <td>${book.author?.encodeAsHTML()}</td>
    <td>${book.pages?.encodeAsHTML()}</td>
    <td>${book.title?.encodeAsHTML()}</td>
  </tr>
</g:each>
```

Notice that each call to encodeAsHTML() uses the null-safe ? operator to make sure you don't get hung up with a NullPointerException. (See Section 3.8, *Safe Dereferencing (?)*, on page 42 for more information.)

In the case of the show action, Book.get pulls the appropriate Book out of the database and passes it to the show.gsp view. The id parameter can be named explicitly—bookstore/book/show?id=1—but Grails will also interpret anything in the PathInfo as an id parameter as well—bookstore/book/show/1. Regardless of how the id is passed in, the book is added to the map and used happily by show.gsp:

```
<tr class="prop">
  <td valign="top" class="name">Id:</td>
  <td valign="top" class="value">${book.id}</td>
</tr>

<tr class="prop">
  <td valign="top" class="name">Author:</td>
  <td valign="top" class="value">${book.author}</td>
</tr>
```

Render

```
def save = {
  def book = new Book(params)
  if(!book.hasErrors() && book.save()) {
    flash.message = "Book ${book.id} created"
    redirect(action:show,id:book.id)
  }
  else {
    render(view:'create',model:[book:book])
  }
}
```

The third R of Grails controllers is perhaps the most versatile of the three. Here in the save action, we see render used to point to a GSP that isn't named save.gsp. As a matter of fact, looking in the grails-app/views/book directory, we can see that save.gsp doesn't even exist. If the book is successfully saved without errors, the save action passes controller over to the show action. The render method can do much more than render GSP pages. In Chapter 12, *Grails and Web Services*, on page 227, we'll see render used to return XML, Atom and RSS feeds, and even Excel spreadsheets.

11.9 Dynamic Scaffolding

```
// grails-app/Controller/PublisherController.groovy
class PublisherController {
  def scaffold = Publisher
}

// grails-app/domain/Publisher.groovy
class Publisher{
  String name
```

```
    String address
    String city
    String state
    String zipcode

    String toString(){
      return name
    }
}
```

In Section 11.2, *Creating Your First Grails App*, on page 197, you typed grails generate-all Book to create controllers and views for the Book model. This is helpful because it produces files that you can explore while you are learning Grails.

But the real power of Grails is on display when you begin dynamically scaffolding your controllers and views. In a single line—def scaffold = Publisher—you're asking Grails to create the controller and views in memory at runtime. This is incredibly useful early in the process when your domain classes are still taking shape. You're more apt to add a few new attributes here and drop a couple there if you don't have to constantly keep rebuilding the views. The dynamic scaffolding becomes even more valuable when you discover that you can selectively override controller actions and views. If you add your own save action to PublisherController (say, to automatically add a timestamp to the record), all other actions will continue to behave as they normally do. If you want a special look and feel for list.gsp, add that file to the views directory.

Changing the Field Order

```
class Publisher{
  static constraints = {
    name()
    address()
    city()
    state()
    zipcode()
  }

  String name
  String address
  String city
  String state
  String zipcode

  String toString(){
    return name
  }
}
```

Figure 11.5: GRAILS ALPHABETIZES DYNAMICALLY SCAFFOLDED FIELDS.

When you first look at your dynamically scaffolded views, you might be taken aback. Absent any other instructions, Grails alphabetizes your fields in the views. (See Figure 11.5.) At first blush that may seem half-again too clever, but the order of the fields in a JavaBean is *not* defined by the order in which they appear in the source code. POJOs and POGOs should be thought of conceptually as a Map of fields rather than a List.

To let Grails know how you'd like the fields to be ordered in all views (list, show, create, and edit), create a static constraints block and list the fields. This might not seem very DRY,[8] but the constraints block is used for more than just field ordering. In Section 11.10, *Validating Your Data*, on the next page, we'll see another use of the constraints block.

---

8. http://en.wikipedia.org/wiki/Don\%27t_repeat_yourself

Making Changes to the Default Templates

```
$ grails install-templates
```

You have the ability to completely customize the look and feel of your scaffolded views and the default behavior of your controllers. Type grails install-templates, and look in src/templates. There you'll find the starter material to adjust things to your heart's content.

11.10 Validating Your Data

```
class Book {
  static constraints = {
    title(blank:false, maxSize:50)
    author(blank:false)
    cover(inList:["Hardback", "Paperback", "PDF"])
    pages(min:0, max:1500)
    category(inList:["", "Technical", "Fiction", "Non-fiction"])
    excerpt(maxSize:5000)
  }

  String title
  String author
  Integer pages
  String cover = "Paperback"
  String category
  String excerpt

  String toString(){
    "${title} by ${author}"
  }
}
```

Here we see the full power of the static constraints block. It not only controls the field order of the dynamically scaffolded views (as discussed in Section 11.9, *Changing the Field Order*, on page 215), but it also allows you to validate data entry.

Grails supports a number of standard validations. Here are the most popular of the bunch. (See the online Grails Validation Reference[9] for all the possible validation options.)

---

9. http://grails.org/Validation+Reference

Setting	Value	What It Does
blank	true | false	*Prevents empty fields*
email	true | false	*Checks for well-formed email addresses*
inList	["a", "b", "c"]	*Displays a combo box*
min, max	number	*Minimum, maximum value for a numeric field*
minSize, maxSize	number	*Minimum, maximum length for a text field*
unique	true | false	*Prevents duplicate values in database*

Methods such as book.save() validate the object before saving it. (See Section 11.8, *Render*, on page 214 to see this in action.) You can also call book.validate() if you want to check the validation yourself without saving to the database.

```
if(book.validate()) {
  // do something
}
else {
  book.errors.allErrors.each {
    println it
  }
}
```

Now that you have some validation in place, you have a fighting chance of keeping those silly users from trying to create Books with -1 pages. (See Figure 11.6, on the facing page.)

In grails-app/views/book/create.gsp, there is a block of code that looks for errors and displays them in the web page:

```
<g:hasErrors bean="${book}">
  <div class="errors">
    <g:renderErrors bean="${book}" as="list" />
  </div>
</g:hasErrors>
```

Custom Validation Messages

```
// grails-app/i18n/messages.properties
default.invalid.min.message=Property [{0}] of class [{1}]
        with value [{2}] is less than minimum value [{3}]

// your custom message
book.pages.min.notmet=Who are you trying to kid?
                      No book could have [{2}] pages.
```

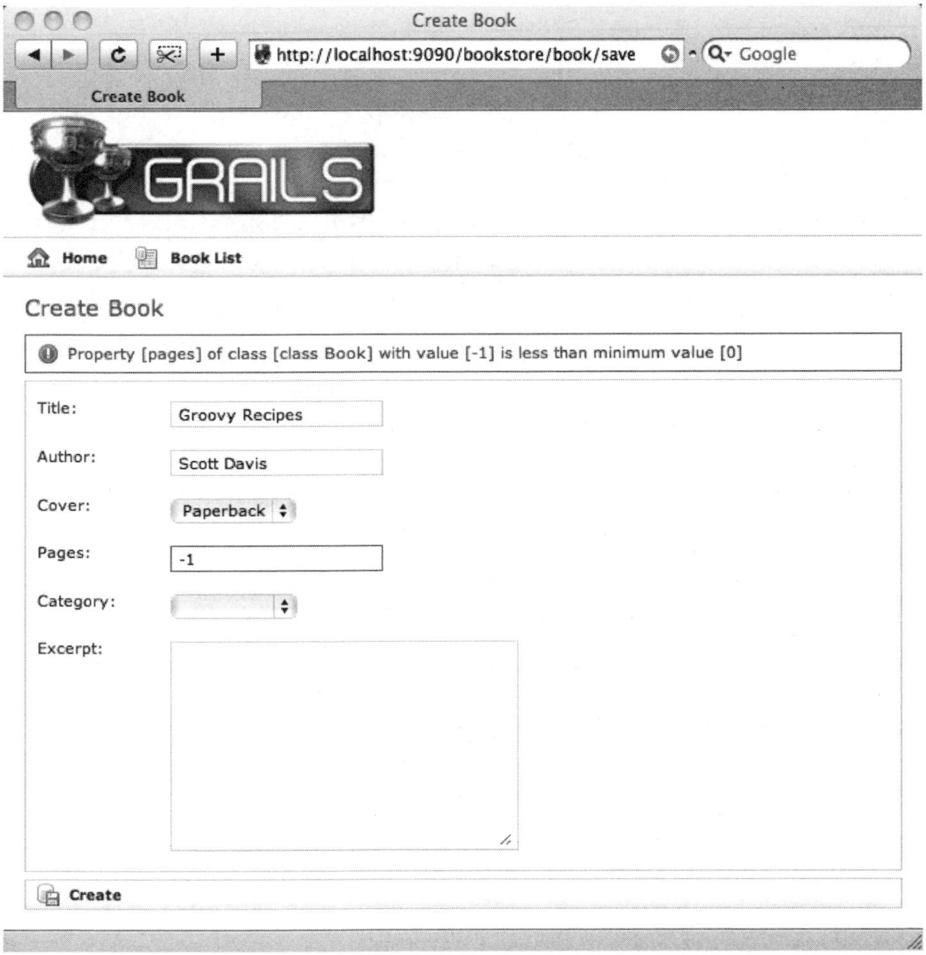

Figure 11.6: GRAILS VALIDATION

All the standard error messages are internationalized and stored in Java properties files in grails-app/i18n. You can make a change here, and the error message will be changed throughout the application.

To further internationalize your Grails application, install the i18n Templates plug-in by typing grails install-plugin i18n-templates. For more on this plug-in, see the online reference material.[10] For more on plug-ins in general, see Section 12.6, *Installing Plug-Ins*, on page 241.

You can supply a custom error message per domain class per field by adding it to messages.properties. The property key varies slightly from the default keys. Here is a list of the customization keys for the standard validations listed earlier. Again, see the online Grails Validation Reference[11] for all the possible validation message codes.

Setting	Value
blank	*className.propertyName.blank*
email	*className.propertyName.email.invalid*
inList	*className.propertyName.not.inList*
max	*className.propertyName.max.exceeded*
maxSize	*className.propertyName.maxSize.exceeded*
min	*className.propertyName.min.notmet*
minSize	*className.propertyName.minSize.notmet*
unique	*className.propertyName.unique*

11.11 Managing Table Relationships

```
static hasMany = [books:Book]
static belongsTo = [publisher:Publisher]
```

With these two little phrases—hasMany and belongsTo—you can model table relationships with ease. Let's see some one-to-many, one-to-one, and many-to-many relationships in action.

One-to-Many Relationships

```
// grails-app/domain/Publisher.groovy
class Publisher{
  static constraints = {
    name()
  }
```

---

10. http://grails.org/I18n+Templates+Plugin
11. http://grails.org/Validation+Reference

```
    static hasMany = [books:Book]

    String name

    String toString(){
      return name
    }
}

// grails-app/domain/Book.groovy
class Book {
  static constraints = {
    title()
    author()
    pages()
    publisher()
  }

  static belongsTo = [publisher:Publisher]

  String title
  String author
  Integer pages

  String toString(){
    "${title} by ${author}"
  }
}
```

A Publisher wouldn't be much of a Publisher if it offered only one Book. So it goes to follow that *one* Publisher needs to have *many* Books. Notice the static hasMany line in Publisher.groovy. This is a Map, since a good Publisher might also have *many* Editors, *many* Distributors, and so on.

To make the connection on the Book side of the equation, add a corresponding static belongsTo. Now you might be thinking that you should create an Integer field for the Publisher.id. In fact, that is exactly how the tables get linked in the database behind the scenes. But by adding the Publisher class, we are using the more Java-centric Composition pattern. GORM will deal with loading up the Book class with values from separate tables transparently.

This also allows you to use GPath and drill into the Publisher class from Book, like println book.publisher.name. For more on GPath, see Section 7.2, *Understanding the Difference Between XmlParser and XmlSlurper,* on page 108.

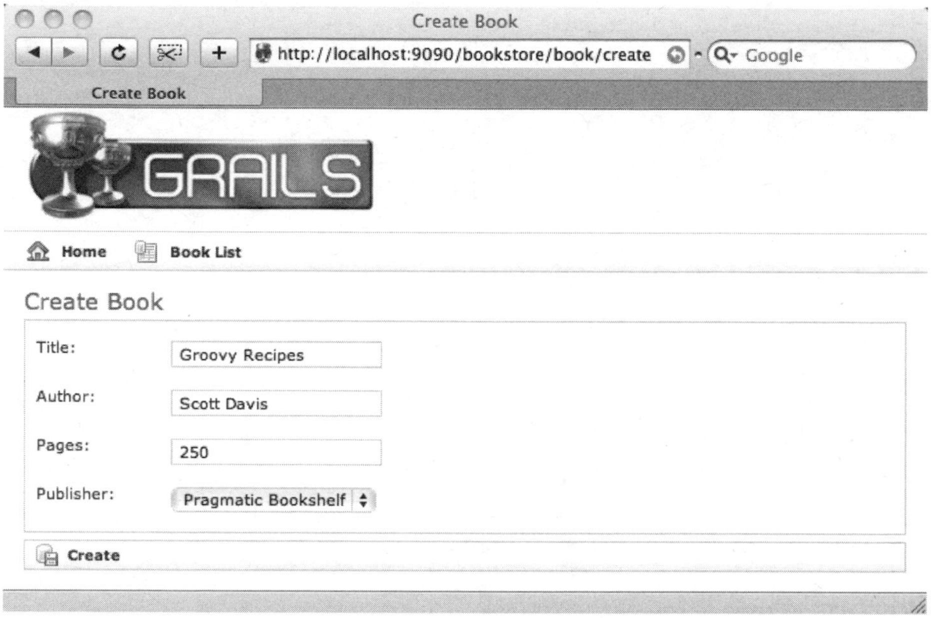

Figure 11.7: One-to-many relationships

GORM takes care of the back-end database work for you, and the dynamic scaffolding discussed in Section 11.9, *Dynamic Scaffolding*, on page 214 does a great job of visually representing this relationship between Book and Publisher. (See Figure 11.7.) The Publisher field is a combo box populated by the Publisher table. The value that appears in the combo box is the toString method.

With just a static hasMany=[books:Book] on the *one* side and a Publisher publisher field declaration on the *many* side, you have created a 1:M relationship between Publisher and Book. However, if you delete a given Publisher, all the associated Books will be left as orphans in the database. If you want to enforce cascading deletes and updates, specify static belongsTo = Publisher in Book.

One-to-One Relationships

```
// grails-app/domain/Author.groovy
class Author{
  static constraints = {
    name()
    address()
  }
```

```
    String name
    Address address

    String toString(){
      return name
    }
}

// grails-app/domain/Address.groovy
class Address{
  static constraints = {
    street()
    city()
    state()
    zipcode()
  }

  String street
  String city
  String state
  String zipcode

  String toString(){
    return "${street}, ${city}, ${state}, ${zipcode}"
  }
}
```

Continuing with the book example, let's examine the authors. They have to live somewhere, but only the lucky few can afford more than one house. It's a pretty safe bet that you can model Author and Address as a 1:1 relationship.

Just giving the Author an Address field creates the 1:1 relationship. As with a 1:M relationship, the Author table has an Address.id field, but GORM presents you with the full object upon request. In Figure 11.8, on the next page, you can see how Grails portrays the relationship in HTML. Again, the toString method of Address is used to populate the combo box.

Technically, what you have in place at this point is not a true 1:1 relationship since there is nothing stopping another Author from living at the same Address. Adding a unique constraint as discussed in Section 11.10, *Validating Your Data*, on page 217 closes this loophole.

If you want to maintain Author and Address as separate classes but save them both to the same table, you can do this by adding static embedded = ["address"] to the Author class. GORM will create fields like address_street and address_city to guard against name collisions in the embedded class.

Figure 11.8: ONE-TO-ONE RELATIONSHIP

Many-to-Many Relationships

```
// grails-app/domain/Book.groovy
class Book {
  static belongsTo = Author
  static hasMany = [authors:Author]

  String title
  Author author
}

// grails-app/domain/Author.groovy
class Author {
  static hasMany = [books:Book]

  String name
}
```

At this point, many-to-many relationships should be no surprise. GORM creates a third association table and adds a foreign key back to both Book and Author. Unfortunately, the dynamic scaffolding won't model this relationship in HTML. You are left to write your own GSP pages. Some clever soul might create a ManyToMany plug-in to help with this, so keep your eyes open for developments on this front.

11.12 Mapping Classes to Legacy Databases

```
class Magazine{
  String title
  String editorInChief

  static mapping = {
    table 'periodical'
    columns {
      id column:'periodical_id'
      title column:'publication_name'
      editorInChief column:'person_in_charge'
    }
  }
}
```

Developing a new application from scratch is a lot of fun, but many times you must deal with legacy applications. In this situation, you might be tempted to name your classes and fields to match the existing tables. Although this isn't a bad strategy, you can also use a *static mapping* block to link your class names to table names, as well as attribute names to column names. See the online ORM DSL Guide[12] for all the details.

---

12. http://grails.org/GORM+-+Mapping+DSL

Chapter 12

Grails and Web Services

The Grails framework can be used for far more than just plain old HTML. In this chapter, we'll explore RESTful web services, JSON web services, Atom feeds, podcast feeds, and more. Heck, you can even return Excel spreadsheets from a Grails application if you want.

12.1 Returning XML

```
import grails.converters.*

class BookController {
  // return a single book as xml
  def showXml = {
    render Book.get( params.id ) as XML
  }

  // return a list of books as xml
  def listXml = {
    def list = Book.list(params)
    render(contentType:"text/xml"){
      books{
        for(b in list){
          book(id:b.id){
            title(b.title)
            author(b.author)
            pages(b.pages)
            unescaped << "<!-- coverPrice is coming in the next version -->"
}}}}}}
```

In Section 11.8, *Render*, on page 214, we used render to return a partial GSP fragment. In this example, we use two different forms of render to return well-formed XML. If you are a fan of RESTful web services (as discussed in Section 9.3, *RESTful GET Requests*, on page 150), you can see how easy it is to get started down that path with Grails.

Render as XML

```
// return a single book as xml
def showXml = {
  render Book.get( params.id ) as XML
}
```

```
<book id="1">
  <author>Scott Davis</author>
  <pages>250</pages>
  <title>Groovy Recipes</title>
</book>
```

The standard show method renders a POGO in a GSP page. The showXml method here demonstrates how to return XML instead. As long as you remember to import grails.converters.* at the top of the file, you can simply render any POGO as XML.

If you have wget installed on your system (it comes standard on Linux, Unix, Mac OS X; you can download[1] it for Windows), you can test this by typing wget "http://localhost:8080/bookstore/book/showXml/1". You can, of course, also visit that URL in your web browser.

In this example, we'll leave off the parentheses on the render method to make it feel more like a DSL. See Section 3.3, *Optional Parentheses*, on page 34 for more information.

Render Using a StreamingMarkupBuilder

```
// return a list of books as xml
def listXml = {
  def list = Book.list(params)
  render(contentType:"text/xml"){
    books{
      for(b in list){
        book(id:b.id){
          title(b.title)
          author(b.author)
          pages(b.pages)
          unescaped << "<!-- coverPrice is coming in the next version -->"
}}}}}
```

---

1. http://www.gnu.org/software/wget/

```
<books>
  <book id='1'>
    <title>Groovy Recipes</title>
    <author>Scott Davis</author>
    <pages>250</pages>
    <!-- coverPrice is coming in the next version -->
  </book>
  <book id='2'>
    <title>GIS for Web Developers</title>
    <author>Scott Davis</author>
    <pages>255</pages>
    <!-- coverPrice is coming in the next version -->
  </book>
</books>
```

If you want to customize the XML output in any way—ignore certain fields, render some of the data as attributes instead of elements, and so on—you can use the alternate form of render demonstrated in listXml. Since as XML won't work on ArrayLists, converting a list of POGOs to XML requires this extended form of render.

You first pass in contentType:"text/xml" to the render method. contentType can be any valid MIME type. Next, you use the included Streaming-MarkupBuilder to emit your XML. (See Section 8.12, *StreamingMarkup-Builder at a Glance*, on page 136 for more information.) Typing wget "http://localhost:8080/bookstore/book/listXml" allows you to test the output.

12.2 Returning JSON

```
import grails.converters.*

class BookController {
  // return a single book as json
  def showJson = {
    render Book.get( params.id ) as JSON
  }

  // return a list of books as json
  def listJson = {
    def list = Book.list(params) as Book[]
    render list as JSON
  }
}
```

If you've done any web development recently, you've probably come across JavaScript Object Notation (JSON).[2] Parsing complex XML in the

---

2. http://en.wikipedia.org/wiki/Json

browser can be a slow and tedious process. JSON avoids the problem by returning native JavaScript objects. One simple eval, and you have a well-formed JavaScript object ready for use. http://json.org has pointers to support libraries implemented in dozens of languages other than JavaScript, but you don't need 'em in Grails. The same as XML syntax you see in Section 12.1, *Returning XML*, on page 227 can be used here as JSON.

Render as JSON

```
// return a single book as json
def showJson = {
  render Book.get( params.id ) as JSON
}
```

```
{"id":1,
  "class":"Book",
  "author":"Scott Davis",
  "pages":250,
  "title":"Groovy Recipes"
}
```

The standard show method renders a POGO in a GSP page. The showJson method here demonstrates how to return JSON instead. As long as you remember to import grails.converters.* at the top of the file, you can simply render any POGO as JSON.

If you have wget installed on your system (it comes standard on Linux, Unix, Mac OS X; you can download[3] it for Windows), you can test this by typing wget "http://localhost:8080/bookstore/book/showJson/1". You can, of course, also visit that URL in your web browser.

In this example, we're leaving off the parentheses on the render method to make it feel more like a DSL. See Section 3.3, *Optional Parentheses*, on page 34 for more information.

Rendering a JSON List

```
// return a list of books as json
def listJson = {
  def list = Book.list(params) as Book[]
  render list as JSON
}
```

```
[
  {"id":1,
```

---

3. http://www.gnu.org/software/wget/

```
      "class":"Book",
      "author":"Scott Davis",
      "pages":250,
      "title":"Groovy Recipes"},
    {"id":2,
      "class":"Book",
      "author":"Scott Davis",
      "pages":255,
      "title":"GIS for Web Developers"}
]
```

Using the as JSON converter works on arrays as well. Notice that you must convert the ArrayList of books to an array for this to work. (See Section 3.14, *List Shortcuts*, on page 48 for more information.)

Typing wget "http://localhost:8080/bookstore/book/listJson" will allow you to test the output.

12.3 Returning an Excel Spreadsheet

```
class BookController {
  def listExcel = {
    def list = Book.list(params)
    render(contentType:"application/vnd.ms-excel") {
      html{
        body{
          h1("Books")
          table{
            // table header
            tr{
              th("ID")
              th("Title")
              th("Author")
              th("Pages")
            }

            //table body
            for(b in list) {
              tr{
                td(b.id)
                td(b.title)
                td(b.author)
                td(b.pages)
}}}}}}}}
```

This is actually possible thanks to Microsoft Excel's ability to render HTML and a little bit of HTTP trickery. You start by building a straightforward HTML document using render's embedded Streaming-MarkupBuilder. (See Section 8.12, *StreamingMarkupBuilder at a Glance*,

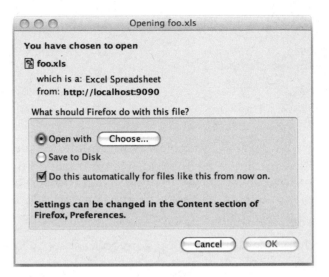

Figure 12.1: SAVING EXCEL SPREADSHEETS FROM GRAILS

on page 136 for more information.) For a more complex spreadsheet, you might have better luck creating a grails-app/views/listExcel.gsp file. This document is simple enough that I chose to render it inline here.

If you set the contentType to text/html, the web browser will dutifully render the page itself. (Feel free to try this.) Since you're explicitly telling the browser that this is an Excel document, the browser passes it off to the appropriate viewer. Visit http://localhost:8080/bookstore/book/listExcel in your web browser. If you are using Internet Explorer, the spreadsheet will show up right in the browser. If you are using Firefox or Safari, Excel should launch in a separate window. Neat, eh?

You can use this trick for more than just spreadsheets. If the application in question understands HTML, try passing in the appropriate MIME type[4] and see what happens.

Also bear in mind that you don't even have to be running Grails to take advantage of this. I've done this sort of thing plenty of times from plain old Groovlets. (See Section 2.6, *Running Groovy on a Web Server (Groovlets)*, on page 22 for more information.)

---

4. http://www.iana.org/assignments/media-types/

Saving the Spreadsheet as an Attachment

```
def listExcel = {
  def list = Book.list(params)
  response.setHeader("Content-Disposition", "attachment; filename=foo.xls")
  render(contentType:"application/vnd.ms-excel") {
    ...
  }
}
```

With one more bit of HTTP tomfoolery, you can induce the web browser
to display a Save As dialog box instead of actually rendering the spreadsheet. (See Figure 12.1, on the facing page.) The Content-Disposition
header is a hint to the browser. It says to treat this response as an
attachment named foo.xls.

12.4 Setting Up an Atom Feed

```
class ItemController {
  def atom = {
    def itemList = Item.list( params )
    def df = new java.text.SimpleDateFormat("yyyy-MM-dd'T'HH:mm:ss'-07:00'")

    // feed header
    def updated = df.format(itemList[0].datePosted)
    def feedHeader = """<feed xmlns="http://www.w3.org/2005/Atom">
      <title type="text">aboutGroovy.com</title>
      <updated>${updated}</updated>

      ...
    """

    // feed body
    StringBuffer feed = new StringBuffer()
    itemList.each{item ->
      def sw = new java.io.StringWriter()
      def x = new groovy.xml.MarkupBuilder(sw)
      x.entry(xmlns:"http://www.w3.org/2005/Atom"){
        author{name("Scott Davis")}
        published(df.format(item.datePosted))
        ...
      }
      feed.append(sw.toString() + "\n")
    }

    // feed footer
    def feedFooter = "</feed>"

    response.setContentType("application/atom+xml")
    render "${feedHeader}${feed}${feedFooter}"
  }
}
```

The code we see here has been in production at AboutGroovy.com for several years. It is battle-tested and quite stable. It takes the brute-force approach to generating Atom since when I originally wrote it the plug-in infrastructure was just a twinkle in Graeme Rocher's eye. (Graeme is the founder and tech lead of the Grails project.)

There is a constant stream of new and exciting software coming from the Grails plug-in community. (See Section 12.6, *Installing Plug-Ins*, on page 241.) Something might get released next week that makes this code look clunky and obsolete. (It wouldn't be tough to do.)

However, by avoiding external dependencies, this code has proven to be remarkably resilient across Groovy upgrades, Grails upgrades, and everything else. That alone speaks volumes about the power of *learning a specification* versus *learning a library* that manages the specification on your behalf. Atom is a reasonably simple format with plenty of good documentation.[5]

Part 1: The Setup

```
def atom = {
  params.max = 10
  params.sort = 'datePosted'
  params.order = 'desc'
  def itemList = Item.list( params )
  def df = new java.text.SimpleDateFormat("yyyy-MM-dd'T'HH:mm:ss'-07:00'")

  // feed header
  ...
  // feed body
  ...
  // feed footer
  ...
}
```

The first thing you do is pull the Items out of the table and put them in itemList. Since syndication feeds usually show the most recent items first, you sort the list by item.datePosted in descending order.

Speaking of dates, Atom requires all dates to appear in the RFC 3339[6] format. The SimpleDateFormatter gives you a single class that you can reuse throughout this method.

---

5.   http://en.wikipedia.org/wiki/Atom_\%28standard\%29
6.   http://www.ietf.org/rfc/rfc3339.txt

Part 2: The Header

```
def atom = {
  ...

  // feed header
  def updated = df.format(itemList[0].datePosted)
  def feedHeader = """<feed xmlns="http://www.w3.org/2005/Atom">
    <title type="text">aboutGroovy.com</title>
    <link rel="alternate" type="text/html" href="http://aboutGroovy.com"/>
    <link rel="self" type="application/atom+xml"
         href="http://aboutGroovy.com/item/atom" />
    <updated>${updated}</updated>
    <author><name>Scott Davis</name></author>
    <id>tag:aboutgroovy.com,2006-12-18:thisIsUnique</id>
    <generator uri="http://aboutGroovy.com" version="0.0.2">
      Hand-rolled Grails code
    </generator>
  """

  // feed body
  ...
  // feed footer
  ...
}
```

The header is largely boilerplate text. The only variable is updated,
which you pull from the most recent entry in the list and format using
the SimpleDateFormatter.

Part 3: The Body

```
def atom = {
  // feed header
  ...

  // feed body
  StringBuffer feed = new StringBuffer()
  itemList.each{item ->
    def sw = new java.io.StringWriter()
    def x = new groovy.xml.MarkupBuilder(sw)
    x.entry(xmlns:"http://www.w3.org/2005/Atom"){
      author{name("Scott Davis")}
      published(df.format(item.datePosted))
      updated(df.format(item.datePosted))
      link(href:"http://aboutGroovy.com/item/show/${item.id}",
        rel:"alternate", title:item.title, type:"text/html")
      id("tag:aboutgroovy.com,2006:/item/show/${item.id}")
      title(type:"text", item.title)
      content(type:"xhtml"){
        div(xmlns:"http://www.w3.org/1999/xhtml"){
          p("Category: ${item.type}")
```

```
            p{a(href:item.url, "Original Source")}
            p(item.shortDescription)
            p(item.description)
          }
        }
      }
      feed.append(sw.toString() + "\n")
    }

    // feed footer
    ...
```

This is arguably the most important block of code in the method. You walk through each Item in the list and create the Atom <entry>. You fake out the namespace in the MarkupBuilder. At some point I should probably refactor this to be a true namespace, but it works for now. (See Section 8.7, *Creating Namespaced XML Using StreamingMarkup-Builder*, on page 133 for more information.) This is arguably the most important block of code in the method. You walk through each Item in the list and create the Atom <entry>. You fake out the namespace in the MarkupBuilder. At some point I should probably refactor this to be a true namespace, but it works for now. (See Section 8.7, *Creating Namespaced XML Using StreamingMarkupBuilder*, on page 133 for more information.)

Here is the Item domain class:

```
class Item {
  static constraints = {
    title(blank:false)
    type(inList:['news', 'event', 'media'])
    shortDescription(maxSize:255)
    description(maxSize:4000)
    url(blank:false)
    postedBy()
    datePosted()
  }

  String url
  String title
  String shortDescription
  String description
  String type
  Date datePosted
  Integer postedBy

  String toString(){
    return "$type: $title"
  }
}
```

Part 4: Rendering the Result

```
def atom = {
  // feed header
  ...
  // feed body
  ...

  // feed footer
  def feedFooter = "</feed>"
      response.setContentType("application/atom+xml")
      render "${feedHeader}${feed}${feedFooter}"
}
```

In this final block of code, you close up the feed element, set the ContentType to application/atom+xml, and render the three strings together as a single response. In Section 9.13, *Parsing an Atom Feed*, on page 168, we can see what the resulting XML document looks like.

12.5 Setting Up an RSS Feed for Podcasts

```
class PodcastController {
  def rss = {
    def itemList = Podcast.list( params )
    def df = new java.text.SimpleDateFormat("yyyy-MM-dd'T'HH:mm:ss'-07:00'")

    // feed header
    def updated = df.format(itemList[0].datePosted)
    def feedHeader = """
    <rss xmlns:itunes="http://www.itunes.com/dtds/podcast-1.0.dtd"
         version="2.0">
    <channel>
      <title>About Groovy Podcasts</title>
      <link>http://aboutGroovy.com</link>
      ...
    """

    // feed body
    StringBuffer feed = new StringBuffer()
    itemList.each{item ->
      def tmp = """<item>
      <title>${item.title}</title>
      <itunes:author>Scott Davis</itunes:author>
      <enclosure url="${item.url}"
                 length="${item.fileSize}" type="audio/mpeg" />
      ...
      """
      feed.append(tmp + "\n")
    }
```

```
        // feed footer
        def feedFooter = "</channel></rss>"

        response.setContentType("text/xml")
        render "${feedHeader}${feed}${feedFooter}"
    }
}
```

If you read Section 12.4, *Setting Up an Atom Feed*, on page 233, this example should look remarkably similar. The mechanics of putting together a text-based Atom feed are no different from putting together a podcast feed. Only the dialect is different.

Apple provides a thorough set of online documentation[7] to guide you through the RSS dialect required for a well-formed podcast feed.

Part 1: The Setup

```
def rss = {
  params.max = 10
  params.sort = 'datePosted'
  params.order = 'desc'
  def itemList = Podcast.list( params )
  def df = new java.text.SimpleDateFormat("yyyy-MM-dd'T'HH:mm:ss'-07:00'")

  // feed header
  ...
  // feed body
  ...
  // feed footer
  ...
}
```

You first pull the Podcasts out of the table and put them in itemList. Since syndication feeds usually show the most recent items first, you sort the list by podcast.datePosted in descending order.

Speaking of dates, all dates should appear in the RFC 3339[8] format. The SimpleDateFormatter gives you a single class that you can reuse throughout this method.

---

7. http://www.apple.com/itunes/store/podcaststechspecs.html
8. http://www.ietf.org/rfc/rfc3339.txt

Part 2: The Header

```
def rss = {
  ...

  // feed header
  def feedHeader = """
<rss xmlns:itunes="http://www.itunes.com/dtds/podcast-1.0.dtd"
     version="2.0">
<channel>
  <title>About Groovy Podcasts</title>
  <link>http://aboutGroovy.com</link>
  <language>en-us</language>
  <copyright>2007 AboutGroovy.com</copyright>
  <itunes:subtitle>
    Your source for the very latest Groovy and Grails news
  </itunes:subtitle>
  <itunes:author>Scott Davis</itunes:author>
  <itunes:summary>About Groovy interviews</itunes:summary>
  <description>About Groovy interviews</description>
  <itunes:owner>
    <itunes:name>Scott Davis</itunes:name>
    <itunes:email>scott@aboutGroovy.com</itunes:email>
  </itunes:owner>
  <itunes:image href="http://aboutgroovy.com/images/aboutGroovy3.png" />
  <itunes:category text="Technology" />
  <itunes:category text="Java" />
  <itunes:category text="Groovy" />
  <itunes:category text="Grails" />
  """

  // feed body
  ...
  // feed footer
  ...
}
```

The header is completely boilerplate text. There is not a single variable bit of information.

Part 3: The Body

```
def rss = {
  // feed header
  ...

  // feed body
  StringBuffer feed = new StringBuffer()
  itemList.each{item ->
    def tmp = """<item>
    <title>${item.title}</title>
```

```
        <itunes:author>Scott Davis</itunes:author>
        <itunes:subtitle></itunes:subtitle>
        <itunes:summary>${item.shortDescription}</itunes:summary>
        <enclosure url="${item.url}" length="${item.fileSize}" type="audio/mpeg" />
        <guid>${item.url}</guid>
        <pubDate>${df.format(item.datePosted)}</pubDate>
        <itunes:duration>${item.duration}</itunes:duration>
        <itunes:keywords>java,groovy,grails</itunes:keywords>
        </item>
        """
        feed.append(tmp + "\n")
    }


    // feed footer
    ...
```

This is arguably the most important block of code in the method. In it, you walk through each Podcast in the list and create the RSS <item>. In Section 12.4, *Setting Up an Atom Feed*, on page 233, we used a Markup-Builder to build the body. In this case, you just use a simple GString. (Scandalous, isn't it?)

Here is the Podcast domain class:

```
class Podcast {
  static constraints = {
    title(blank:false)
    shortDescription(maxSize:255)
    description(maxSize:4000)
    url(blank:false)
    fileSize()
    duration()
    postedBy()
    datePosted()
  }

  String url
  String title
  String shortDescription
  String description
  Date datePosted
  Integer postedBy
  Integer fileSize
  String duration

  String toString(){
    return "$title"
  }
}
```

Part 4: Rendering the Result

```
def rss = {
  // feed header
  ...
  // feed body
  ...

  // feed footer
  def feedFooter = "</channel></rss>"
  response.setContentType("text/xml")
  render "${feedHeader}${feed}${feedFooter}"
}
```

In this final block of code, you close up the rss element, set the ContentType to text/xml, and render the three strings together as a single response. In Section 9.14, *Parsing an RSS Feed*, on page 169, we can see what the resulting XML document looks like.

12.6 Installing Plug-Ins

```
$ grails list-plugins
$ grails install-plugin [NAME]
```

The real power of Grails comes from its vibrant, community-driven plug-in system. Visit http://grails.org/Plugins or type grails list-plugins to get an idea of the different ways that Grails can be extended. There are plug-ins that add SOAP and XML-RPC support. Flash and Google Web Toolkit clients can be developed as an alternate to Groovy Server Pages. Acegi and JSecurity can be used for security-minded sites. Plug-ins for Captchas can keep spambots out of your public forums. The Searchable plug-in brings in Lucene to enable Google-like searches. The list of available plug-ins is ever growing and limited only by the creativity and enthusiasm of the Grails community.

Index

D

E

F

G

Web 2.0

Welcome to the Web, version 2.0. You need some help to tame the wild technologies out there. Start with *Prototype and script.aculo.us*, a book about two libraries that will make your JavaScript life much easier.

See how to reach the largest possible web audience with *The Accessible Web*.

Prototype and script.aculo.us

Tired of getting swamped in the nitty-gritty of cross-browser, Web 2.0–grade JavaScript? Get back in the game with Prototype and script.aculo.us, two extremely popular JavaScript libraries that make it a walk in the park. Be it Ajax, drag and drop, autocompletion, advanced visual effects, or many other great features, all you need is write one or two lines of script that look so good they could almost pass for Ruby code!

Prototype and script.aculo.us: You never knew JavaScript could do this!
Christophe Porteneuve
(330 pages) ISBN: 1-934356-01-8. $34.95
http://pragprog.com/titles/cppsu

The Accessible Web

The 2000 U.S. Census revealed that 12% of the population is severely disabled. Sometime in the next two decades, one in five Americans will be older than 65. Section 508 of the Americans with Disabilities Act requires your website to provide *equivalent access* to all potential users. But beyond the law, it is both good manners and good business to make your site accessible to everyone. This book shows you how to design sites that excel for all audiences.

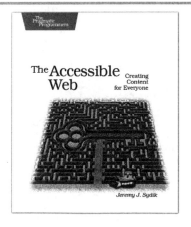

The Accessible Web
Jeremy Sydik
(304 pages) ISBN: 1-934356-02-6. $34.95
http://pragprog.com/titles/jsaccess

The Pragmatic Bookshelf

The Pragmatic Bookshelf features books written by developers for developers. The titles continue the well-known Pragmatic Programmer style and continue to garner awards and rave reviews. As development gets more and more difficult, the Pragmatic Programmers will be there with more titles and products to help you stay on top of your game.

Visit Us Online

Groovy Recipes's Home Page
http://pragprog.com/titles/sdgrvr
Source code from this book, errata, and other resources. Come give us feedback, too!

Register for Updates
http://pragprog.com/updates
Be notified when updates and new books become available.

Join the Community
http://pragprog.com/community
Read our weblogs, join our online discussions, participate in our mailing list, interact with our wiki, and benefit from the experience of other Pragmatic Programmers.

New and Noteworthy
http://pragprog.com/news
Check out the latest pragmatic developments in the news.

Save on the PDF

Save on the PDF version of this book. Owning the paper version of this book entitles you to purchase the PDF version at a terrific discount. The PDF is great for carrying around on your laptop. It's hyperlinked, has color, and is fully searchable.

Buy it now at pragprog.com/coupon.

Contact Us

Phone Orders:	1-800-699-PROG (+1 919 847 3884)
Online Orders:	www.pragprog.com/catalog
Customer Service:	orders@pragprog.com
Non-English Versions:	translations@pragprog.com
Pragmatic Teaching:	academic@pragprog.com
Author Proposals:	proposals@pragprog.com